Teachers Can Be Financially Fit

Tawni Hunt Ferrarini • M. Scott Niederjohn
Mark C. Schug • William C. Wood

Teachers Can Be Financially Fit

Economists' Advice for Educators

 Springer

Tawni Hunt Ferrarini
Plaster School of Business
and Entrepreneurship
Lindenwood University
St Charles, MO, USA

Mark C. Schug
University of Wisconsin–Milwaukee
Milwaukee, WI, USA

M. Scott Niederjohn
Lakeland University
Plymouth, WI, USA

William C. Wood
James Madison University
Harrisonburg, VA, USA

ISBN 978-3-030-49355-4   ISBN 978-3-030-49356-1   (eBook)
https://doi.org/10.1007/978-3-030-49356-1

This Springer imprint is published by the registered company Springer Nature Switzerland AG
The registered company address is: Gewerbestrasse 11, 6330 Cham, Switzerland

Preface

We want you to learn how to practice sound financial principles so that you can live securely and comfortably—that's why we have written this book.

We are educators and you are educators, attracted to the teaching profession for numerous reasons. Many of us wish to work with young people, others of us love our subject areas, or both. Prospective teachers enter the profession believing it offers a certain level of job security and good benefits, usually including a defined-benefit, state-funded pension. The job security and benefits become more important as teachers remain in the profession.

But things are changing. Pensions vary widely from state to state and even within school districts. Some states, such as Illinois, New Jersey, and California, have not kept pace with their pension obligations. Moreover, knowledge that a state pension awaits them in retirement may make teachers inattentive about planning aggressively for a financially sound future.

Teachers in private schools face greater difficulties in saving for retirement. Many private schools do not offer even basic 403(b) saving plans, and when they do, they are often not very generous. Much the same can be said of many charter schools and private colleges and universities.

Research indicates that teachers are not well served by the financial services industry. For example, Tara Siegel Bernard (2016) argues that teachers do not get high-quality financial advice. All too often, after learning why they might set up a 403(b) plan to boost their standard of living in retirement, teachers are then steered into high cost annuities and never learn of investment options with lower costs and higher returns. Now the Securities and Exchange Commission is investigating to determine whether violations of federal securities regulations have occurred.

What Teachers Tell Us

In preparation for writing this book, we have talked to a great many teachers. They have told us that they believe that they can become financially secure but added that it isn't going to be easy. Hard choices are involved. Several doubt that teachers can become financially secure based solely on their own income. Many feel that additional income is needed from spouses and second jobs. Others stress problems related to high levels of college debt. One teacher commented to us: "Most teachers I know, especially single ones, tend to live almost paycheck to paycheck…"

We do continuing education for teachers as part of our regular jobs, and we often hear about teachers' top financial worries. They're not so much concerned about managing their own finances but they worry about the long term. We often hear that becoming financially secure is becoming more and more of a challenge.

What are teachers' top financial worries? Most often we hear that veteran teachers are concerned about maintaining a good standard of living in retirement. Young teachers and even those still working on their degrees are concerned about their standard of living—everything from paying off student loans to wondering whether they will ever be able to afford a home. Other concerns we hear are paying children's college tuition, credit card debt, too much debt, health, inadequate emergency funds, and health insurance. Whether the economy is good or bad, a few worry about facing an economic downturn or even a financial collapse.

Many of the teachers we meet work part-time jobs to help them achieve their goals. Some of these "side hustles" are teaching-related such as camp counselor, curriculum writer, coach, and college teacher. But many part-time jobs were not education-related, such as bartender, construction worker, Uber driver, and waitress.

While teachers seem to have many of the same financial concerns as others, they also face some distinctive challenges. They believe they need to make special sacrifices to achieve their financial goals. They regard their compensation as less than adequate. Public school teachers count on state pension plans for retirement. Private and charter schoolteachers face challenges of their own. Retirement issues stand out, as do other financial worries such as managing debt and having adequate savings.

This book is designed specifically for teachers seeking to improve their overall probability of success while reducing the likelihood of financial stress—whether you teach in a public school, private school, charter school, or higher education setting.

And though the purpose of this book is to help you with your financial life, as economists we are always interested in the extra benefits that flow to others ("positive externalities"). In this case, such externalities may occur when you pass along the knowledge from this book to the students you teach. This might occur in a formal financial literacy course, but it could occur in any setting. These important life skills are relevant to most any field or area where you engage students.

In this book each chapter has a common structure, opening with a teacher case study. A narrative explaining key concepts and topics follows. Concrete examples of how to apply the concepts are infused throughout. A brief overview of the content concludes the narrative. Then we present supplementary material through questions likely to be asked by teachers, together with our concise answers. Each chapter concludes with a "Financial 911," focusing on a financial emergency related to the chapter topic. We explain how to address such emergencies while living and working as a teacher.

We have organized this book into 14 chapters. In all of the chapter-opening case studies, the experiences described are real, though we have changed names for privacy reasons and some details to make the points clearer. But in every case the math works.

In Chap. 1, you will meet Makayla, a lifetime educator who achieved a striking degree of financial success and was able to leave a continuing impact on her community.

In Chap. 2 you will meet Liam, who follows the lead of Ethel, the school custodian, to start his journey toward financial health.

In Chap. 3, Eric finds a way to take advantage of his teaching job to retire early and pursue other income-earning opportunities.

In Chap. 4, Terry and Megan choose different transportation alternatives—and Megan increases her lifetime wealth a quarter of a million dollars as a result. We'll show you how Megan's very ordinary strategy can increase your wealth more than you might have imagined.

Chapter 5's case study is about Clayton and Katrina, who learn that home ownership is a good financial move for them. At the same time, they learn to avoid the financial pitfalls of home ownership and they see why home ownership may not be for everyone.

In Chap. 6, Jose, a school human resources director, finds out that some of his staff members are facing major financial problems brought on by unwise use of credit. This chapter de-mystifies credit reports and explains how credit can be from heaven or from hell.

In Chap. 7, Emma has an amazing day. She learns that she is inheriting $20,000 from her grandmother's estate—that's the good news. The bad news is that she now must decide what to do with it. As someone with knowledge about high tech, she faces a possibility of making errors out of overconfidence, but in this chapter she learns three rules of building wealth for the long term while avoiding common pitfalls.

In Chap. 8, Tom turns out to be terrific in getting a comfortable retirement. Tom did not go into teaching to become rich, but it turns out that by making a series of good choices he has assured a comfortable retirement for himself and his family. Tom learns how to manage three key sources of income: state retirement, Social Security, and personal investments.

Chapter 9's case study introduces us to Donna, a fabulous charter school math teacher with a teacher savings retirement problem. After teaching for 15 years, Donna barely has anything to show financially for her teaching work so far. In Chap. 9 she learns about tax-advantaged savings options that can help.

In Chap. 10's case study, we meet Margaret, who is worried about her student loans and her future as an instructor in higher education. Margaret was off to a promising start in her first full-time job after getting a Ph.D., but then the reality of her student loan balance hit home.

Chapter 11's case study features Jayden and Alyssa, who do everything right about insurance but end up getting it wrong. They spend a lot of money on different types of coverage and they never suffer a big loss, and yet their wealth is well below what it could have been with better choices.

In Chap. 12, Penelope suffers a crisis unexpectedly—the loss of her husband in an accident. Nothing could have prepared her for that. And yet with sound money management and a smart relocation, Penelope finds a secure job to go on to successfully raise her son and send him to college. There was no getting around the initial loss, but Penelope and her son do find happiness.

Chapter 13's case study follows the story of Maria, who saw true poverty while serving as a Peace Corps teacher in a distant country. When she gets back, Maria learns that what makes nations prosperous is not what she expected. Understanding the basics of a market economy is important for all citizens, but particularly for those interested in making good financial choices.

In Chap. 14, we learn that Anthony's spectacular success as a multimillion-dollar entrepreneur had modest roots—an activity in his middle school classroom. Anthony's teacher Mrs. Seneca led students through the basics of sound money management and what it takes to launch a successful business. More importantly, Mrs. Seneca encouraged Anthony to take control of his own future.

That's where we're going. For now, the most important thing is for you to believe that you can do this. If you believe you can never improve your financial situation, and you make poor choices as a result, then your pessimistic belief will come true. Teachers are prone to commiserate with each other about the fact that they don't make much money. Compared with other professions, it is true that teachers frequently earn less income. But as you will discover, teachers can be financially fit.

Reference

Siegel Bernard, Tara. (October 23, 2016) Think Your Retirement Is Bad? Talk to a Teacher. New York Times: Your Money https://www.nytimes.com/2016/10/23/your-money/403-b-retirement-plans-fees-teachers.html

St Charles, MO, USA   Tawni Hunt Ferrarini
Plymouth, WI, USA   M. Scott Niederjohn
Milwaukee, WI, USA   Mark C. Schug
Harrisonburg, VA, USA   William C. Wood

Contents

1

Yes, Teachers Can Be Financially Fit

1.1 Teacher Case Study: Makayla, the Unexpected Philanthropist

Makayla worked as a high school chemistry teacher for 40 years. She took a great deal of pride in her former students' accomplishments, including the student who became her family physician. This student started out as one of the shy girls in the corner of the chemistry lab, but under Makayla's instruction and encouragement became both a chemistry star and a school leader. After graduating from medical school, Makayla's student came home to practice medicine while also starting a small free clinic. Makayla became one of the clinic's most faithful donors. When Makayla retired to a sunny coast, she was missed at the clinic, but not forgotten.

In fact, Makayla is still remembered at the clinic today. When her will was read, a startled small audience in the law office heard that she was leaving $1.2 million to the clinic. With Makayla's gift, the clinic has funded research, provided care for those who could not pay, and inspired even more young students from Makayla's town to study nursing and medicine.

Makayla's big donation was especially surprising because she had lived in a modest ranch home located within a mile of the school. She never flaunted her money. No one suspected she had the kind of money to retire comfortably, move to a warm climate for her golden years, and still have enough left to care for herself and leave a major inheritance. How had she accumulated so much wealth on a teacher's salary? If you are curious about the answer, this book is for you.

© The Editor(s) (if applicable) and The Author(s), under exclusive license to Springer Nature Switzerland AG 2021
T. Hunt Ferrarini et al., *Teachers Can Be Financially Fit*,
https://doi.org/10.1007/978-3-030-49356-1_1

1.2   It's Not All About the Money; It's About Happiness

They say money buys happiness. Is that true? In many ways, we think the answer is "yes." Money allows you to pursue what you value most in life. Money helps with taking good care of all of the people that you care about. It allows you to contribute to your children's education, see your friends, or even one day take your family on a luxury cruise. The point is not that money buys happiness—but instead that it enables and supports strong ties to other people, which is a key to happiness. For most people, the things they highly value are their family, friends, and children. With sound finances, you can enjoy all this and more.

When you have made good choices in life and earned and saved your money, you feel a deep sense of satisfaction. We're not writing this book to make you rich, but rather to make you happy and comfortable. When experts assess the unhappiness of major life events, such as divorce and health crises, financial problems loom large. Financial stress can negatively affect nearly every facet of our lives including:

- Marital relationships.
- Parents' relationships with their children.
- Physical health, with problems that can include lack of sleep, heart problems, or chronic illness.
- Mental health, with problems that can include anxiety, depression, or even suicide.

Financial security, in contrast, promotes happier, more fulfilling, lives.

Teachers, like some others, sometimes think that becoming wealthy means being greedy, ruthless or maybe dishonest. If this is you, we suggest that you get the greed thing out of your system. Doing good things such as donating to charity or educating the next generation will require wealth to make it happen. The desire to build wealth and eventually become financially independent does not make you greedy. If you use the money you make for greedy ends, then, sure, you can be considered greedy. But what if this financial success allows you to help your church, donate to those less fortunate, help a family member with a medical crisis or just spend more time with your family? Who could argue with such aspirations?

This book says that teachers can be financially fit—but you'll quickly learn that we do not favor single-mindedly chasing after money until you have a million dollars saved up. Instead, we favor a balanced life in which money serves you and you do not serve money. If you heed the advice in the following chapters, you will find yourself comfortable with budgeting and spending. You will find that you don't stress about big financial decisions and that you're insured against disaster. You will be more confident about investing and saving for your retirement. And, you will know a little more about how a market economy operates.

Among people who achieve a high degree of financial security, teachers are surprisingly well represented. How did so many teachers achieve financial success, given that teacher pay is notoriously lower than pay in other professions? The answers lie not in the amount of money these teachers took home in their paychecks, but in the choices they made in putting that money to work.

1.3   Finding a Financial Adviser

Although you can get a good start on your financial goals with the advice in this book, it won't be long before you need the help of a financial adviser. Here are some important things to remember as you think about getting financial advice:

- We recommend fee-based financial planners. As the name implies, these advisers provide advice in exchange for a fee. Other financial planners get a commission – that is, a percentage of the amount you invest. Although commissioned financial planners can seem to be "free," in the required disclosures you'll see that they are getting their cut. Financial planners deserve to get paid and will get paid. The question is how. In our experience it works better to pay the fee openly rather than have it occur through commissions. To find a fee-based financial planner near you, visit the National Association of Personal Financial Advisers (http://napfa.org).
- This next point is delicate: Be careful if someone comes to your school as a financial adviser but only has insurance-based financial products and services to offer. (This person may even be a retired former teaching colleague or social contact – that's why it's delicate.) To do the best, you need to be working with advisers that can handle the whole range of financial services, especially the mutual funds we will explain fully in Chap. 7. Insurance has a place in your financial future (see Chap. 11), but insurance-based financial products have definite drawbacks as investments. Choosing these insurance-based products because of friendship or other ties can literally cost you tens of thousands of dollars of lifetime wealth.

- In our experience (verified by many unbiased financial advisers), it's best not to keep large sums of money in the bank. The deposit accounts banks offer are indispensable and their Certificates of Deposit (CDs) are safe, but these assets do not grow in the long term as much as the other assets we will explain in this book. In particular, if you have large amounts of long-term or retirement savings in CDs, you are probably making a mistake. If your only financial advice comes from someone who works at a bank, that is not a good sign. Our advice is to use your bank for banking but not for investing.
- Ask around. Other teachers will have experience with financial advisers and can provide recommendations. Remember, however, that someone with only unfavorable options for you (such as high-commission insurance offerings) can be quite charming. Stick to well-established fee-based financial planners.
- Pay attention to how you're treated when you inquire about an initial meeting with a financial planning professional. If the front office takes a long time returning phone calls or brushes off your questions, it probably won't get better when you have invested your money.
- It's important to understand what a financial adviser can and can't do for you. A financial adviser can help you refine your goals and help you set up the accounts to get there. The adviser can help you review your progress, avoid unnecessary taxes, and keep you posted on changes in the law that may affect you. But a financial adviser can't make goals for you or make you stick with the discipline that it takes to have money to invest.

1.4   The Scorecard: Net Worth

Although money is not everything, having enough money is important. How do you keep score? The best single measure of financial well-being is *net worth*. This is defined as your assets minus your liabilities. To calculate your net worth, add up the value of everything you own—maybe just a car if you're starting out, maybe a lot more if you have a house and investments. Then you subtract off the value of everything you owe, such as car loans, mortgages, student loans, credit card debt, and so forth. The result, what you own minus what you owe, is your net worth.

If you make good choices, over time your net worth will grow. You may be starting from a shocking low level of net worth. The four authors of this book all started out with negative net worth and eventually achieved a level of financial success. If all you own is a $2000 car and all you owe is $60,000 in student loans, your net worth is ($2000 – $60,000), or a *minus* $58,000. Still, with good choices you can turn your net wealth positive and then just keep going.

Veteran teachers will typically have a positive net worth and some will have net worth in the millions of dollars. If you have a low or negative net worth, now is an excellent time to start moving in the right direction. This book can show you the way.

1.5 Teacher Tip Sheet: Yes, Teachers Can Be Financially Fit

- Can money buy you happiness? Maybe not completely but it sure helps. Being financially fit allows you to do things you love and, more importantly, be with and care for the people you love.
- It's financial stress that contributes to unhappiness including stress on relationships, divorce, mental health, and physical health.
- You may need the help of a financial advisor. Use caution. This is a big decision. We recommend fee-based financial planners.

Keep score by calculating your net worth. Making good choices will help you net worth grow over time. At retirement age, you might be surprised to learn that you became an accidental millionaire.

1.6 Q&A

1. Are you, the authors of this book, rich?
   - Good question. The short answer is yes. We could not feel confident advising you about your finances if the four of us were financial train wrecks. All of us began our careers with negative net worth and all of us have accumulated sufficient wealth for a comfortable lifestyle. More importantly, all of us are grateful for the opportunities we have had in a free society. But are we as rich as Warren Buffett or Bill Gates? No, we are not.
2. What's your background?
   - We are economic educators. We have devoted major parts of our careers to teaching teachers in how to successfully impart economic and finan-

cial knowledge to their students. We have worked with standards-based curricula and have authored instructional materials. We have taught thousands of teachers, sometimes for pay and sometimes as volunteers. We will be the first to say that we do not have all of the financial answers, but we also know enough to confidently tell you about what works and what does not.

1.7   Financial 911 for Teachers

We all know people who are financially successful and others who are living paycheck to paycheck or are loaded with debt. Why are some people financially successful while others struggle? We all know teachers who are in both camps. Even within families, people with the same upbringing, there are some brothers and sisters who do well financially and others who do not. What explains the difference? A theme that runs through this book is that even people of modest means — like most teachers — can be financially fit. How can you or someone you know stop living paycheck to paycheck or reduce debt? It's not *what* you make. It's the *choices* you make.

There are two big steps toward achieving financial success. First, financial fitness begins by understanding a few basic principles. It all starts with living below your means. That is the secret sauce. In order to accomplish anything financially, you have to spend less than you receive. For most of us, that starts with establishing financial goals and setting up a monthly budget. These ideas are explained in Chap. 2. Subsequent chapters offer advice on earning more income, buying a car, buying a home, managing credit and debt, handling risk, and saving and investing for the long term. That is the knowledge part.

The second step is taking action. You need to apply the principles you read. That, of course, is the harder part. While your financial fitness is ultimately up to you, that does not mean you have to go it alone. As discussed earlier, getting a financial advisor can help. Maybe you want to establish a financial fitness club for likeminded colleagues at school. Maybe enroll in a financial planning course at a local community college. Your local community almost certainly has non-profit organizations or church groups that focus on people's financial health. Finally, don't hesitate to contact the authors. We'd love to hear from you. If, for example, you organize a school book club focused on this book, perhaps we can arrange for a virtual meeting or two with one of the authors.

One last thought. Once you get going, you might be surprised how reinforcing the whole journey is. As you see your debt decline, your savings increase and it becomes a self-fulfilling enterprise. The stress eases. You begin to realize that becoming financially successful is well within your grasp.

2

Spending and Saving: A Guide for Teachers

2.1 Teacher Case Study: Liam Discovers Ways to Create Value

Liam was a star football player in high school. He landed a full athletic scholarship at a small private college after graduation. Soon after his arrival on campus, an academic advisor noticed that Liam did not comprehend what he read. At first, Liam pushed back and refused help but only became more frustrated. Eventually he accepted assistance and overcame his learning challenges with the help of many professors. Liam's experience taught him about the importance of learning and helping others overcome their own learning challenges. Liam decided he wanted to be a teacher and completed his degree on time and with good grades.

Unfortunately, Liam did not land a full-time teaching job immediately after graduation. The market was flooded with new teachers and few teachers were retiring. In other words, supply was plentiful and at the time demand was especially limited.

Taking the advice of some seasoned teachers, Liam started substitute teaching at schools with high-risk students. He volunteered to coach, monitor halls, and chaperone events. Very quickly, administrators and veteran teachers noticed. Soon, they began alerting him to upcoming job openings and offering to write strong letters of recommendation. Consequently, Liam landed a full-time teaching job.

Friends and family said that Liam finally realized his dream. However, Liam disagreed. Finding his first full-time job was only a short-term goal. He

© The Editor(s) (if applicable) and The Author(s), under exclusive license to Springer Nature Switzerland AG 2021
T. Hunt Ferrarini et al., *Teachers Can Be Financially Fit*,
https://doi.org/10.1007/978-3-030-49356-1_2

also wanted to go on to be a principal and the head of a charter school. Liam planned to continue to grow and develop within his profession.

At the same time, Liam wanted to live life. For him, that meant marrying his college sweetheart, saving for a down payment to buy a starter house, and having a family. Liam decided a plan was needed. Having not taken any personal finance courses in college or high school, Liam decided to donate time at a local bank sponsoring a community day for seniors. It was at the bank where Liam met Ethel.

Ethel was a custodian from a neighborhood school. With one foot in retirement, she wanted to make sure that all was in order by getting a second opinion from someone other than her school's financial advisor. To Liam's surprise, Ethel was going to retire a millionaire! Yes, her yearly salary as a custodian was less than Liam's teaching salary. What? How did she do that? Liam had to know more.

Ethel's experiences matched common sense. Simply put, common sense says the following: Budget with a plan for life. Save early and often. Spend less than you earn. Avoid debt. And, find someone with financial knowledge to help you make the most out of you're the income you have and the savings you put aside through diversified investments.

2.2   Budgeting for Life: Mapping Out Success

To become financially secure like Ethel, you don't have to win the lottery or leave the teaching profession to find a higher paying job. Teachers taking home $40,000 a year can become millionaires. Following Ethel's example on budgeting, saving, strategic spending, spare use of debt, and diversified investing can make you financially secure.

So let's begin.

2.2.1   Let's Get Started and Set Some Goals

Write down your two biggest lifetime financial dreams. Jot down some ideas and describe the steps to take to make them realities. Just treat this exercise like writing a lesson plan. Every lesson plan starts with objectives. Make yours clear, as shown in Fig. 2.1.

Stating your goals and describing how you plan to reach them are vitally important. How you plan to manage your income, spend, use credit, take out loans, save, and buy and sell assets in order to reach those goals will play a big

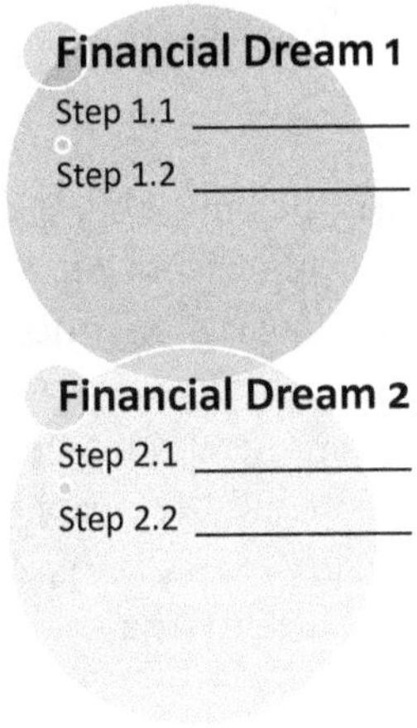

Financial Dream 1

Step 1.1 _____

Step 1.2 _____

Financial Dream 2

Step 2.1 _____

Step 2.2 _____

Fig. 2.1 Financial goals

part in determining if you realize your lifelong dreams. These lifetime goals tell you where you plan to be in 20, 30, or more years as you move closer to retirement and enter your "golden" years. Now is the time to plan for success in order to realize your dreams.

Dreaming big is important but living in the here and now is too. Plus, your big dreams are made up of a series of not-so-big dreams. These are your short-term (up to a year or so) and medium-term goals (between 2 and 5 years.) So, take a few more minutes and list. Include things like:

- Spend less than you bring in on a monthly basis.
- Set up an emergency fund account to handle setbacks.
- Pay off student or car loans.
- Plan a vacation.
- Start a family.
- Live every day with financial security.

Regardless of occupation, work status, or personal preferences, setting sound financial goals and working toward them will help you live a happier and less stressful life. Membership to financial fitness and sound money management is open to everyone. All who are willing to set goals, lay out plans to achieve them, and be disciplined to do what it takes to achieve them will live more securely than those who do not. This is the magic potion, and there is only one golden rule.

2.2.2   Spend Less Than You Earn

So, take a deep breath. No one has to constantly consider leaving teaching for a better paying job. On average, you and other teachers can stay put by spending less than you earn, building up a cushion in your savings, moving pass financial milestones, balancing debt against income, and preparing to retire securely.

Let's get to work, follow Liam's lead, and become Ethel. By design, as a teacher you have fierce dedication and deep passion for whatever you take on. Your profession is peppered with examples that impress the non-teaching world. Take that get-up-and-go, despite-the-odds attitude and channel it into money management.

If you are reading this book, chances are you want to get into financial shape and establish a routine. So, each chapter describes a different aspect of your financial life. Some guidelines are provided for each. Decide what mix of financial guidelines works best for you. Figure out to follow them in order pass important mile markers laid out in this book in order to fulfill your financial dreams.

2.3   Objective: Budget for Life and Analyze Tradeoffs

Regardless of where you are with respect to money management, everything starts with a budget. A budget helps organize your finances, track your spending and savings, evaluate your overall financial health, and map out how to achieve specific goals by rearranging what is happening in your budget.

Gather together all your financial information, the bills you paid over the last month, your last two paychecks, and any property tax or insurance statements paid over the last year.

Start looking for a budget. Use your own spreadsheet, download a budgeting template, or install an app. There is so much from which to choose at no money cost. Use what makes sense to you. For example, one extremely popular website and app is Mint.com. (This is not to be confused with the educational site Mint.org.) Mint.com is free to all users and supported by Intuit, the company behind both TurboTax® and QuickBooks®. Record goals, create and manage a budget, categorize and track spending, get financial tips, receive alerts when you deviate from plans, and keep a pulse on your credit score.

In addition to Mint there is a plethora of other sites and apps with similar features and services, including banks and investment companies. Shop around. Get the right fit and start budgeting for your financial success. Need concrete goals and specific guidelines based on what you enter into your budget? Consider using an app or registering on a website that provides access to advisors. Concrete guidelines exist on how to change different spending, saving, and debt choices in order to reach different goals and pass different financial milestones.

Let's take a look at an example in Table 2.1. Tia entered all household information into a budgeting app with the stated goal of increasing her savings. Review Tia's budget and offer advice.

The example in Table 2.1 shows you how you can treat a personal budget like a worksheet with objectives. With goals in mind, keep track of your income, spending, saving, and debt. Review what happens one month and

Table 2.1 Tia's monthly budget

Monthly Income (after taxes and health insurance)	$ 3000.00
Supplemental income	$ –
Interest earned on savings	$ 4.00
Total Income	$ 3004.00
Fixed Expenses	
Housing/utilities	$ 600.00
Phone and data plan	$ 120.00
Transportation (Car loan)	$ 200.00
Student loan	$ 330.00
Credit card 1 + 2 + 3	$ 136.00
Savings	$ 50.00
Total Fixed Expenses	**$ 1436.00**
Variable Expenses	
Clothing/personal care and services	$ 200.00
Food	$ 900.00
Gas and other auto expenses	$ 120.00
Gym membership and personal trainer	$ 100.00
Household supplies	$ 80.00
Medicine/health supplies	$ 18.00
Entertainment	$ 150.00
Total Variable Expenses	**$ 1568.00**
Total Expenses	**$ 3004.00**
Comparison	
Total cash available	$ 3004.00
Less total expenses	$ 3004.00
Cash balance	$ –

tweak next month to make things happen. It has never been easier to achieve financial goals with today's websites and apps.

In summary, put a budget to work for you. Use it to know where you stand with respect to income, saving, investing, spending, and debt. Notice how less spending today can help you boost savings and investment, spend without debt in the future, and reduce financial anxiety. A commitment to budgeting can also reduce any urge to splurge on credit cards when future tradeoffs are revealed, requiring less personal savings and spending in the future. Let budgeting provide be your road map to realizing your big financial dreams. Plan to take direct paths. Anticipate detours with backup plans to help you get back on track. Future chapters and their 911 s can help you remedy the financial setbacks in life.

2.4   Objective: Maximizing Income and Benefits

Now, it is time to talk salary. On the publication of this book, the average starting salary for teachers was approximately $40,000, and the average salary for public school teachers was about $60,000, according to the Bureau of Labor Statistics' (BLS) Occupational Outlook Handbook. That's about $10,000 less than other professions requiring bachelor's degrees. This reality leads teachers to sometimes feel downtrodden.

They struggle to explain why teacher pay is so low, reasoning that education is a dynamic force behind social and economic development. Research links robust education and investments in human capital to overall economic growth and prosperity across countries and time. More education seems to translate into higher lifetime earnings across occupations. All of this seems very important to thousands, if not millions, of people. So, why are teachers' salaries so low? Why are they not paid more? The simple answer is "It is not personal. It is just economics."

Across the nation, the supply of teachers applying for jobs as K-12 teachers continues to grow faster than demand, on average. This explains why teaching salaries are relatively low. Only when the growth in supply slows relative to demand or growth in demand accelerates faster than supply will teachers' salaries increase (minus the introduction of any government or union considerations).

Step back and look. Some states are seeing teacher salaries rising. This is in response to waves of teachers retiring and others choosing to exit the profession to land higher paying jobs outside of education. It takes time for these factors to work their way into the system.

To see what is going on in your backyard and investigate the trends in your state with respect to the supply of and demand for teacher and their impact on salaries, check out the U.S. Department of Labor's website, CareerOneStop (careeronestop.org). To keep apprised of how what is happening with salaries across the U.S. when all states are considered and project the growth in average openings across schools, visit the Bureau of Labor Statistic's Occupational Outlook Handbook (bls.gov/ooh).

Of course, benefits and other perks also contribute to total teacher compensation. Public school teachers receive higher pay and earn better benefits than private school teachers, on average. Legislation and collective bargaining agreements are given credit. By contrast, private school teachers are less affected by state and local politics. So, they gain more control over their curriculum, engage in less standardized testing, and are better situated to respond to the evolving needs and learning preferences of students. The intrinsic value teachers' place on these types of tradeoffs in overall pay and benefits is not captured by data. Nevertheless, they exist and often influence whether a teacher will fill public or private school teaching positions.

2.4.1 Extra Income

Teachers are well known for being entrepreneurial. Tutoring, coaching, and selling lesson plans during the school year are especially popular. Driving for Uber or Lyft and renting out a room during the summer months can provide extra income and flexibility in the summer months. Jump ahead to Chap. 3 or hop online to explore teacher tested ways to boost and supplement your income.

2.4.2 Saving Regularly: Build a Rainy-Day Fund

Saving serves two very important purposes. It provides you with emergency funds, and it provides funds to take on diversified investments in order to reach other financial goals. Savings for a rainy-day are savings dedicated to covering the expenses associated with the reality that you cannot predict some things. A flat tire in a remote location requires a costly tow. A stove that catches fire can cause serious smoke damage throughout the house. Your phone gets stolen or breaks. You or your spouse get laid off. The list goes on. Stuff just happens.

Prepare for the "stuff." Create a financial cushion to soften the blow of the unexpected financial hardships in life. Let you be the person who gets you through your "rainy days." The last thing you need to worry about when facing a series of unfortunate events is finances. Let what is in your emergency fund provide the financial relief you need so you can channel your energies toward managing the details surrounding the situation.

Experts advise you to have 3–6 months of funds set aside for emergency use. Once you know what you require, on average, to get through a month of expenses start saving for 1 month. Move on to two. Shoot for getting up to 6 months. And then, do not touch these savings.

Place your "rainy day" savings in your budget, treat it as a fixed "expense," and protect it. Draw on it when stuff happens. Eliminate the urge to use a credit card to make a payment if there is any chance that you cannot pay in full by the end of the first billing cycle. Details explaining why are provided in Chap. 6.

2.5   Save Regularly and Invest: Compounding Interest

Albert Einstein gets credit for claiming that compound interest is most powerful force in the universe. It explains how you can put your money to work to earn income without going to work!

Here are some key terms. The money placed in savings is called the *principal*. *Interest* is the amount of money earned on the saved funds or principal. *Compounding* is simply the process by which interest (or the returns on the principal savings) is reinvested to generate additional returns over time.

The rate of interest gives you the percentage of the principal paid interest. For example, an interest rate of seven percent (7%) would pay $7 for every $100 saved in the simplest of situations. *Simple interest* is paid only on the principal. *Compound interest* is paid on the initial principal *plus* any interest earned throughout the life of the deposit (and any additional savings).

Unlike simple interest, compound interest pays interest on interest over the life of the investment. Wow! Very, very nice, don't you think? To make progress toward retiring comfortably while achieving other milestone goals, put savings (and investments) to work through the power of compounding. Give the money you save (and invest) a job. Put it to work and work it hard. The longer you do and the higher the interest rate is, the more interest income and principal you will have in the future and the more you can do.

To predict how long it can take you, on average, to double your savings use the *Rule of 70*. Just divide 70 by the interest rate of choice and find out how many years, on average, it will take to double your savings and the interest earned through the power of compounding interest. For example, if your money is growing at 7%, divide 70 by 7. That is 10. According to the Rule of 70, it will take about 10 years to double any amount saved and held at an interest rate of 7%. Save $2000 this year, expect $4000 in 10 years, on average.

The best news is that you can turn even small amounts of savings into impressive amounts of future income if you start early. Consider the tale of three savers – Xavier, Tyler, and Pat. Xavier was an education major who completed an online class in personal finance. At age 22, he started saving at college graduation. He took $2400 and placed it in a savings account. On being hired as a full-time elementary teacher, he committed to saving $2400 a year until he reached age 67. Over the course of 35 years, he could earn about $184,000 in interest income by following this plan at 7% interest. Tyler was different than Xavier. She wanted to live life while she was young. So, she waited until age 32 to start saving and investing $2400 annually. Pat waited even longer than Tyler. He started at age 52 for reasons unknown. Let's see how these decisions to save regularly at different phases of life will likely work out for each person at a 7% rate of return compounded annually.

As Table 2.2 shows, Xavier ended up with over $350,000 on retirement! Tyler's 10-year wait was relatively expensive, as she ended up with less than half that amount. Pat made the least amount of progress. His total at 67 years of age was just under $67,000. Yes, earning about $30,000 in interest income is better than nothing. But it is a lot less than $270,000 and $102,000.

Online there are a variety of investment and savings calculators that can help you figure out how to reach your financial goals by adjusting your monthly saving amounts at different rates of interest. Take caution. Be

Table 2.2 Compound interest for Xavier, Tyler and Pat (Compound Interest Calculator at Investor.gov, https://www.investor.gov/additional-resources/free-financial-planning-tools/compound-interest-calculator)

Initial investment of $2400 with monthly contributions of $200	Age range	Future value (7%)	Total contributions	Interest income earned
Xavier	22 to 67/35 years	$ 357,392.30	$ 86,400.00	$ 270,992.30
Tyler	32 to 67/25 years	$ 164,823.53	$ 62,400.00	$ 102,423.53
Pat	52 to 67/15 years	$ 66,931.33	$ 38,400.00	$ 28,531.33

realistic about calculating the future value of monthly savings. Use your budget to be practical about the amount you plan to save each month and what you expect the interest rate to be.

Putting the power of compounding interest to work is one of the easiest and most secure ways to generate income throughout your lifetime. Put your creative juices to work. Find ways to cut spending by $5 a day and automatically deposit the monthly total in a diversified investment account. Forget it is there. Doing so will put your savings and any earned interest to work. 24 h a day, 7 days a week, financial institutions will pay you money when you do, on average. More information on savings, investment, and risk and return is provided in Chap. 9.

2.6   Spending Purposefully

Spending to live and living to spend are very different. Spending purposefully, spending less than you earn, and consuming to live lead to financial security and contribute to comfortable living. Spending more than you earn, spending on credit cards that cannot be paid in full, and frivolous spending, especially with borrowed money, cause stress and anxiety. Avoid them. Turn to healthy spending habits.

Take a critical look at your spending. Do what you did for Tia. Discover areas to reduce spending in order to increase savings or to spend less than you earn. Ask for assistance if needed. While taking a hard look at your spending, determine what you need should you be called to go into bare bones spending mode. That mode includes all the fixed expenses with monthly payments that must be met for reasons explained in future chapters. Just know what they are. Be ready to focus on them should you be called into action and have to draw down your emergency savings. Just have an emergency budget that you can use. It will reduce your financial anxiety.

Once budgeting becomes a part of your normal routine, turn to analyzing spending across categories. Take a look at what is happening with respect to data plans, club memberships, music subscriptions, and so forth. Wrap in money spent on weekend entertainment, dining out, premium drinks, personal care services, veterinary bills, and personal items. Get a big picture and take a broad look at your overall spending. Craft a plan that puts you on a creative path of spending with purpose. Reduce spending and borrowing to increase saving and investing. Put the power of compounding to work for you, not against you. Avoid that. Here's why.

Carefully connecting the dots between what you spend on goods and services today with the lost opportunity to save, invest, and earn interest income in the future empowers you. Savings, investments, and any interest income is within your reach. Overtime and with careful planning, your finances can fund college for your children, a down payment on your first home, or a family vacation. Do not place in yourself in the situation where you borrow what Xavier, Tyler, and Pat saved. Rather than being the recipient of all of that interest income you will become the payer! Those loans could be generating assets such as homes and college educations with expected rates of return once interest costs are considered! When you feel the urge to splurge and spend, resist. Help yourself. Lower your credit card limits or freeze your credit cards. Visualize tradeoffs in your budget. Splurge now and decrease savings or investment. That is, figure out how an extra $100 spent on a night out on credit costs you in terms of savings or investing at a rate of 7% in 5, 10, 20, or 30 years.

You do not have to a miserly life. You can live a happy frugal life if done so strategically, creatively, and with the same passion that motivates you to teach. Entertain at home, enjoy a homemade lunch at work, and start a neighborhood car pool. Drop going to the movie theatre and buying the expensive combos of popcorn and soda. Stream movies. Get Netflix, Amazon Prime, or Hulu. Eliminate that expensive service bill. Stash that cash that rewards you when you find some combination things to reduce consumption and increase savings.

2.7 Conclusion: Saving and Spending for Life!

You deserve some Financial Loving Care (FLC). State your financial goals and put use your budget to work to achieve them. That is, devise plans to earn, spend, save, and use credit for a lifetime of happiness and financial security.

2.8 Teacher Tipsheet on Spending and Saving

- Write down your financial goals.
- Use a budget to map out how you plan to reach them.
- Spend less than you earn.
- Treat your personal budget like a worksheet in your financial lesson plan for life.
- Have an emergency savings account that can cover 3–6 months of expenses.

- Put the power of compound interest to work for you by saving, not against you through credit card debt or bad loans.
- Give yourself lots of financial tender loving care (FTLC.)

2.9 Q&A

1. Do I really need to write down my financial goals? Which should I pick first to tackle – my short-, medium-, or long-term goals?
   - Yes, writing down your goals gives credibility to your commitment and helps identify your where you want your finances to take you. Can you imagine teaching a class without objectives? Your finances are no different. So, treat all your goals seriously. Seek professional advice or chat with a trusted advisor about how to realistically line up your goals.
2. Budgeting sounds like too much work. I just don't have a lot of time in my day. Any advice?
   - Just start. Grab a journal or use your phone. Track spending, bills, pay stubs, cash receipts, and credit card bills over a couple of months. Think about your financial dreams and how you can use purposeful budgeting to achieve them. Trust us. You will find the time to carve out time to enter data and actively use that budget.
3. Are budgets just for paying bills?
   - No. They are so much more. In addition to keeping track of and paying bills on time, they track the steps you take to build up an emergency savings account, fund an investment account, and build up an account that will be used to purchase the next vehicle or finance your next vacation without borrowing.
4. What if I can't meet my originally planned budget?
   - Every quarter you should update your budget. Identify your financial strengths and weaknesses. Recognize and take advantage of your financial strengths. Commit to turning one of your weaknesses into a strength. Next month you should do better.
5. Is there any alternative if I just can't make myself write out a budget?
   - Yes. It's not nearly as good, but some teachers report success by identifying monthly spending that can be cut and automatically getting that amount into their savings accounts.

2.10   Financial 911 for Teachers

If you have an increasing credit card balance, you may soon face a financial 911. The signs of danger include:

- Falling behind on paying credit card bills.
- Using credit to make "just for me" purchases when feeling down.
- Using one credit card to pay another credit card balance.

Credit card debt can compound rapidly when you have lingering or increasing balances. What to do? The basic rule is that you have to *spend less than you receive*. Until you do that, you cannot accomplish any financial goal other than spending. The most important thing in such a situation is to start. Do something positive, even if it only a financial baby step like starting to budget.

Chances are your financial institution offers a basic budget online. If you are not comfortable going online with your financial information, grab a budgeting spreadsheet. It is never too late to get started!

While you begin to make progress using the advice in this chapter, be sure to carefully review your credit card statements every month. Pay special attention to charges that are the same each month, like premium TV and internet service packages. If you can reduce or eliminate any such charge, you do better every month by making one decision now.

Work to keep all of your accounts current—and better yet, work to use your credit cards less or eliminate credit card debt entirely over the long term. Meanwhile, review your budget every quarter or so. But above all, don't let increasing credit card balances put you into a financial 911. Notice the early warning signs and take action immediately.

Finally, Chap. 10 offers specific advice on how to pay off student loan debt. The advice offered for student loan debt also applies to other forms of debt such as credit card debt.

3

Earning Extra Income

3.1 Teacher Case Study: Eric's Story

Eric graduated from a selective state university in the Midwest. During his senior year he lived with a group of friends he met during their freshman seminar course. As a group they attended big-time football and basketball games over the 4 years they were together. Rarely, however, did they find themselves in the same courses. Eric was an education major, and he had always dreamed of teaching high school social studies. His roommates were pursuing other majors like engineering, finance, and computer science.

Fast forward the story into their early 30s. Eric married his high school sweetheart and they were blessed with a young family. Eric loved his high school teaching assignments and he had even pursued leadership positions with a number of national academic organizations typically occupied by college professors. In addition, he had just begun serving as the Social Studies Department Chair in his high school—a role typically reserved for more experienced teachers. Eric enjoyed his family and career balance, yet when his buddies organized get-togethers with the old college gang, he occasionally felt a small sense of regret that he chose to become a teacher. He was not proud of this feeling but it occasionally set in as he visited his pals' elaborate homes and heard about their exotic vacations.

Eric, however, knew his sacrifice today would pay off in the future. His school district offered a set of remarkable benefits not generally open to employees in other occupations. If Eric could stick with his chosen field, he had the rare opportunity to retire at near his full salary after thirty years of

© The Editor(s) (if applicable) and The Author(s), under exclusive license to Springer Nature Switzerland AG 2021
T. Hunt Ferrarini et al., *Teachers Can Be Financially Fit*,
https://doi.org/10.1007/978-3-030-49356-1_3

teaching. At the early age of 52 he planned to leave his teaching job and begin a new career leading his state's history teaching association, allowing him to earn the equivalent of two full-time salaries until the day he chooses to truly retire.

3.2   Invest in Yourself

You are likely familiar with the concept of investing in stocks and bonds and a later chapter in this book will say more about that topic. Investment, however, takes many forms. One form is the development of human capital—the knowledge, skills, health, and values that individuals possess. People develop their human capital through formal and informal education. To obtain education, people give up something in the short run (time, effort, or money, for example) in order to gain larger returns (a good job, for example) in the future. This sort of exchange—giving up something now in order to realize gains later—is true of all investment behavior, whether it involves putting money into a mutual fund or putting resources into education. And you have already made this kind of sacrifice to become a teacher. You earned a bachelor's degree and you also likely invested in other professional development opportunities, perhaps to keep your teaching license current.

3.2.1   Investing in Human Capital

There are many ways for you to invest in your own human capital. These ways certainly include formal education (like earning a bachelor's or master's degree from a college or university). Other ways of increasing human capital include work experience, on-the-job training, specialized training courses, and certifications in specific areas. By undertaking any of these activities, you can increase your human capital and your productivity. Increases in human capital are generally associated with higher incomes but, like all investments, they come with risk. In this case, it may be that your new skills don't lead to the payoff you are hoping for, but you can mitigate this risk by researching programs and institutions of higher education that best fit your career aspirations.

It may be that your school district maintains a salary schedule that provides an automatic jump in pay if you earn an advanced degree. However, it is also true that by earning an advanced degree you generally increase your skills and productivity making you more in demand to other employers. In addition, with each degree you earn, your skills become more specialized and scarce, leading to a smaller supply of those that can do what you can. Carefully weigh the costs and benefits of this decision—that is, will the increased future income from the additional credential earn enough extra income to justify the cost (in dollars and time) of obtaining the degree? If you decide to work toward an advanced degree you will have to decide which field to obtain it in. Many teachers choose to pursue graduate degree at a school of education. This may make sense if you aspire to a career in school administration like a principal or even superintendent. However, you may also prefer to obtain an advanced degree in your field, like history, English, or mathematics. Keep in mind that if you are hoping to use your degree to earn extra income teaching college courses as an adjunct instructor, most accrediting bodies in higher education now require that faculty have a degree (or at least eighteen graduate credits) above the level of students they are teaching.

3.2.2 Comparative Advantage

Perhaps most importantly, try to determine what your comparative advantage is and pursue that in a graduate program. Are you a great teacher that loves pedagogy and working with young people? Are you a good leader that your colleagues look up to and place in positions of influence? When you consider your own interests, aptitudes, and goals, you are asking where your comparative advantage lies. You will be better off if you are really good at something that is highly valued by others. The best major for you takes both elements into account: (1) your own relative talents and (2) how highly these talents are valued by others, as signaled by earnings in your possible fields of study.

3.3 Part-Time Work

Perhaps you just want to earn a little extra income for some spending money, to save for a vacation, or to put away in savings. Your consistent school schedule may make you an ideal candidate for part-time work.

First, think about the areas where you have specialized skills. Could you tutor students outside of school for extra income? Could you help kids prepare for college entrance exams? Perhaps editing or copywriting books or articles could earn some extra money. What about scoring Advanced Placement exams in your field?

Other teachers have chosen to take part-time jobs in fields like retail. Another idea that teachers have taken advantage of is driving for Uber or Lyft.

These opportunities afford you maximum flexibility and the most money is available to be made on busy weekend evenings when you almost certainly won't need to be at school. Other teachers have chosen to take driving fares when it is convenient for them. For example, perhaps you need to provide transportation for your elderly parent to a medical appointment. Could you pick up a couple of fares instead of sitting in a doctor's waiting room?

3.4   Try Your Hand as an Entrepreneur

Even if you aren't in the business department at your school you still could start your own business on the side. Many teachers have done just this in an effort to generate new income. But don't feel you have to limit yourself to businesses based upon your role as a teacher. Many teachers have started other kinds of businesses, perhaps taking advantage of the time they have in the summer to dedicate to such an endeavor. The definition of an *entrepreneur* is *one who innovates and takes risks in developing a product or business*. There are obviously costs and benefits to being an entrepreneur. Entrepreneurs tend to work long hours as they are getting their businesses started and many business ideas fail. While entrepreneurs do not have the security of an employer to provide their health care benefits and help them save for retirement, you likely have that risk covered through your teaching position, so you might be in an ideal position to try out a business idea. Some examples of businesses started by real teachers include:

- A world history teacher started a business taking students and other teachers to Europe in the summer months and this turned into a full-blown travel agency.
- A teacher started a concession stand business at a popular summer festival that has turned into a concession management business that makes him more than his teaching position.
- A teacher that was also an avid outdoorsman created a line of hunting and fishing-related board games that have become quite popular.
- A teacher started a very successful painting business. One day he was painting his own home and neighbor noticed what a nice job he was doing and remarked that he wished he had the time to paint his home. This gave him the idea to start a summer painting business that became a business even more lucrative than his first love of teaching.

3.5   Tips for Starting a Business

Starting a successful business takes time, effort, diligence, and planning. Thankfully there are many resources to helping you get off to a good start. Local universities are likely to have a small business center and other community-based groups of volunteers exist to assist the technical aspects like writing a business plan, accounting and financial issues, or marketing. Starting a business also involves risk. It might make sense to both start small and first try working for someone in the area you want to follow. For example, if you think you could run a summer painting company, start by taking a job as a painter to see if you actually enjoy and are successful at the work.

The U.S. Small Business Administration identifies a set of steps[1] that should be considered before starting a business. Keep these in mind as you research other resources to get started.

1. Write a Business Plan
   - Many templates can be found online but a good plan should include a market analysis, organization, sales strategy, financial requirements, among other important topics.
2. Get Business Assistance and Training
   - Take advantage of free training and counseling services, from preparing a business plan and securing financing, to expanding or relocating a business.
3. Choose a Business Location
   - Get advice on how to select a customer-friendly location and comply with zoning laws.
4. Finance Your Business
   - Investigate loans, venture capital and research grants to help you get started.
5. Determine the Legal Structure of Your Business
   - Decide which form of ownership is best for you: sole proprietorship, partnership, Limited Liability Company (LLC), corporation, S corporation, nonprofit or cooperative.
6. Register a Business Name ("Doing Business As")
   - Register your business name with your state government.
7. Get a Tax Identification Number
   - Learn which tax identification number you'll need to obtain from the IRS and your state revenue agency.

---

[1] www.sba.gov/content/follow-these-steps-starting-business

8. Register for State and Local Taxes
   - Register with your state to obtain a tax identification number, workers' compensation, unemployment and disability insurance.
9. Obtain Business Licenses and Permits
   - Get a list of federal, state and local licenses and permits required for your business.
10. Understand Employer Responsibilities
    - Learn the legal steps you need to take to hire employees.

If you do not find yourself discouraged by this list and are determined to do what it takes to start your own business, you may have what it takes to be a successful entrepreneur.

3.6   You May Need to Move

Almost certainly you have developed close relationships with your fellow teachers in your building as well as the students and their families. This supportive social environment is one of the wonderful aspects of the teaching profession. Unfortunately, however, it may be that to earn more income you might need to consider changing schools. It is just a fact that some districts pay more than others. Further, you can expect public school districts to offer higher salaries than private or charter schools. While this may not always be the case, the salary differential is likely to be particularly acute between public schools and religiously-based private schools. It is very easy to compare the salaries of the public school districts in your area as this information is a public record and frequently on the district's web pages.

3.7   Conclusion: Teachers and Income

Perhaps because teachers hear they are underpaid so often, they just accept it as a fact and don't consider ways to improve their incomes. If teachers take note of the advantages they have—like excellent retirement and health care benefits, a flexible schedule, and lots of time off in the summer—it may be possible to significantly enhance their income. Consider additional educational opportunities that may enhance the pay at your school or allow you to teach courses at a local college. Consider ways to use your teaching skills to earn extra income through tutoring, test preparation, or test scoring. Or, if you think have an idea for a business, don't be afraid to give it a try. Perhaps start small over a summer and see where it takes you. Lastly, while moving to a new school can present challenges it may present another way to increase your income.

3.8 Teacher Tipsheet: Earning More Income

- Consider ways to increase your human capital through advanced education or other professional development opportunities.
- If you decide to begin a graduate degree be sure you have a goal in mind. It could be that you want to move into academic administration or you may want to broaden your opportunities in your academic discipline.
- Consider earning extra income by leveraging your teaching skills. This may mean taking on some extra hours tutoring or helping students prepare for college entry exams.
- Evaluate whether you might want to try your hand at being an entrepreneur. You may be able to take advantage of your summer vacation and excellent benefits to make this a possibility.
- Don't forget that all school districts don't offer the same salary. One way to earn more income may be to move to a new school.

3.9 Q&A

1. Should all teachers pursue an advanced degree?
   - No! Like any decision, the choice to start a graduate program should be evaluated based upon costs and benefits. The costs will include the tuition, books, and fees you will have to pay to take classes. But an even larger cost is time you will spend pursuing this degree that you could have spent on other activities or even working another part-time job. The benefits may include an increase in salary, opportunities to earn more income by moving into administration or teaching classes at a university and, of course, the enjoyment you may feel in learning new knowledge and skills.
2. Should I obtain a master's degree in education?
   - It depends. If you are hoping to improve your income by moving into the administration of your school that might be a good choice. A master's program's in educational leadership may help you become an assistant principal, principal or, perhaps someday, a superintendent. Other

teachers may prefer to remain in a teaching role and could use a master's degree to earn more income by becoming the department chair or teaching classes at a local college or university. Remember that most institutions of higher education will require you to have a master's degree in the field you want to teach.

3. Can I really start my own business?
   - Yes. Many teachers have started successful business. You may have ideas for a business that is based on your teaching skills or the discipline you specialize in. But many teachers have started seemingly unrelated businesses that have turned out to be successful. Remember that challenges facing many entrepreneurs include no access to benefits and a lack of time to pursue their idea. You may be able to keep your teaching benefits while using your summer vacation time to see if your idea for a new business is viable.

4. Are you telling me I have to work in the summer?
   - Probably. It may be possible to develop a business that built around the academic year. However, if you want to maximize the earning potential of your work you will likely need to work in the summer when you likely have the most time. Understand that this is just a tradeoff that you will have to evaluate. One of the great things about the teaching profession is having the flexible summer to pursue other interests. So one opportunity cost of starting a business in the summer is fewer fun summer days with nothing to do but go to the beach.

3.10   Financial 911 for Teachers

You have a financial 911 when your teaching position is eliminated. This can happen when school districts face major budget shortfalls or as the demographics in a community change. Here are things to consider should you find yourself in this unfortunate situation:

- Get ahead of any deadlines, such as those required to file for unemployment compensation. This is not something that you want to put off.
- Meet with your human resources department to be sure you understand the terms of your separation from the district. You may be owed salary for vacation, sick, or personal days you did not take. You also need to know how long you will be covered by your district's health insurance.

- Network with teachers you know in other schools to see if there might be openings. A recommendation from a teacher already in the school can go a long way.
- Spend some time updating your resume. Be sure to add new accomplishments since the last time you needed this document, such as recent professional development opportunities completed.

If you're finding it difficult to obtain a new full-time job quickly, consider substitute teaching or taking other non-teaching jobs in the short-term. And if moving is an option for you, take a look at the parts of the country that are experiencing teacher shortages.

4

Teachers' Wheels: Cars and Transportation

4.1 Teacher Case Study: Different Car Paths for Terry and Megan

When new teachers Terry and Megan drove into the lot at J. Frank Pence Middle School for the first back-to-school meeting in August, they had one thing in common: a $349 monthly car payment. Everything else about their car strategies was different.

Terry was driving a brand-new luxury sport utility vehicle. Getting together the up-front money had not been easy, but then a 36-month lease did the trick. Terry could afford more car by going with a lease instead of a regular auto loan. Megan was still driving the modest sedan she had bought in her last year of college. Her 36-month car loan was just barely affordable, but with help from part-time and summer earnings she made it work.

Terry expected to continue to lease new vehicles as time went by. A teacher's salary wouldn't permit a lot of extras, but the lease made this an affordable luxury. Megan's strategy was different. She planned to pay off that car and take advantage of not having a car payment for some months or years.

Everyone in your building knows a "Terry" and a "Megan." What you might not know is that Megan's strategy will create a quarter of a million extra dollars in lifetime wealth for her! How can that be? It's the power of compound interest. If you arrange things right, you can have a great car and no car payment—freeing thousands and thousands of dollars for wealth building. This chapter shows how.

T. Hunt Ferrarini et al., *Teachers Can Be Financially Fit*, https://doi.org/10.1007/978-3-030-49356-1_4

4.2   A Love Affair?

There is some truth in the saying that we have a "love affair with the automobile." Any of us can give in to car fever when the feelings are strong. We can spend way too much, and then after buying, fall in love with a different new car. Can teachers do better with car purchases? We think so. We believe that teachers can get excellent transportation at a low overall cost—not by radically different behavior, but by making sensible car choices over time.

The best place to start is with an honest assessment of (1) what you must have in a car and (2) what's optional (nice to have if you can afford it but not essential). Some states' economics learning standards refer to this as the difference between "needs" and "wants."

In our opening case study, Terry started out her bad choices by being unsure about her needs. That made Terry susceptible to smooth talk from a dealership sales rep. "You've got to be there for your students no matter what," the sales rep said, selling the reliability of the brand and its all-weather all-wheel drive. "And you need an affordable payment," the sales rep said in selling the lease.

Clearly teachers must be there for their students and must come up with something affordable—but that doesn't mean leasing a luxury sport-utility. Let's have a closer look.

4.2.1   You've Got to Be There

People are counting on you at school. Reliable transportation is a must. That doesn't mean you have to spend a lot, especially when you consider the social environment of your workplace. For most teachers, the school is highly supportive and highly social. Most of the school workforce works very similar hours. This means that, unlike a consultant or repair technician who might have to go anywhere, anytime, teachers likely have access to many friends willing to lend a ride when necessary. Further, most teachers work for employers that are among the quickest to close in bad weather. Usually the buses have to be able to run for school to be in session. This makes teachers unlikely candidates to require all-wheel drive. So while you want reliable transportation, you don't have to take extreme measures to get it.

It's also true that for most teachers, cars are not a closely tracked status symbol. Terry got a few compliments about her new car here and there, but not many people at Terry's school could tell you who drove what into the parking lot. No one would get ridiculed for driving an older but properly maintained used car.

All of this says that teachers should concentrate on the practical side of getting around when they make decisions on cars and transportation. Think about what's vital. Where do you plan to go, with how many people, carrying what cargo? Most often, those transportation requirements are quite modest and not difficult to fill. It's not necessary to have a pickup truck if you're going to get a big load of gardening supplies one time a year.

Beyond the basics, think about what you want and why you want it. This is a great exercise for any educator who is already focused on a fast car or a rugged sport-utility. If you narrow the field too fast, you may make a bad choice. In fact, the most important rule for not making bad deals on vehicles is this: Don't make car decisions in a hurry. Here are some good questions to ask yourself:

- Will it cost a lot to operate the vehicle I'm considering? Good gas mileage will reduce fuel costs, but there are a lot of other costs such as maintenance to consider also. Some cars, especially luxury brands, may have expensive replacement tires and other components.
- Will it cost a lot to insure the vehicle I'm considering? The more expensive the car, in general, the more expensive it will be to insure.
- How many people, and how much cargo, do I need to carry – and where am I going? It may be nice to be able to take eight people into the wilderness with all-wheel drive, but that will cost a lot. The money will not be well spent if you usually carry smaller loads to tamer locations.

None of this is to say you shouldn't drive what you like. As you can afford it, a better car becomes one of many competing possibilities for your money. The problem is that many educators get trapped into expensive car solutions without looking hard at the alternatives.

4.2.2   The "Happy-o-Stat" Applied to Cars

Several places in this book we refer to the "happy-o-stat," a casual name for the way that newly purchased items become routine after a while and then provide less satisfaction. The analogy is with a thermostat. It senses that inside room temperature is getting cold and kicks the heating system on until it warms up.

In a similar way, you may feel great just after buying something nice like a new car. But as you drive it to school and back day after day, it begins to feel routine. Your happy-o-stat kicks in, and your level of satisfaction declines to normal. If someone asked you, "How satisfied are you with your car on a scale of 1 to 5?" it might well have been "4" for your old car and, in time, just "4" for a new car with lots of bells and whistles.

Knowing in advance that your happy-o-stat will kick in, you can make better car-buying decisions. Carefully consider which characteristics will continue to provide happiness, as opposed to things like those custom wheels that look great in the showroom but, over time, become "just wheels."

4.3   The Wealth-Building Power of Good Car Choices

Our opening case study claimed that Megan's simple car-buying choices would bring her $250,000 in greater lifetime wealth than Terry's choices. How can that be? Here are some of the reasons Megan's strategy works so much better.

Megan will pay off her car in just over two more years because she got good advice and followed it. That advice was never to buy a car that took more than 36 months to pay off. When she put "36 months" and the advertised interest rate into an online payment calculator, she found she could only afford a $12,000 car. That price range got her a nice but not great 5-year-old used car from a reliable brand with 60,000 miles.

After paying off her car, Megan is planning to continue making a car payment! —not to the credit union where she borrowed the money, but to her own savings account. If she does that steadily for 5 years, she'll then have a 12-year-old used car with about 150,000 miles plus about $24,000 saved for a newer car (at 5% return for 5 years). She can then move up to a nicer used car. By continuing to make a $349 car payment to herself, she can build thousands and hundreds of thousands of dollars' worth of lifetime wealth.

But how about Terry? Terry finds that, having started out with a lease, she's never in a position to do anything other than lease. Her lease has her paying rent every month on her car. At the end of her first lease, 36 months, she had no value built up — and in fact found that she owed 25 cents per mile for "excess mileage" beyond 10,000. To avoid those penalties, she would have needed to drive under 200 miles a week, including commuting and all of those road trips. The dealership rolled her mileage penalty into the next lease.

That made her monthly payment go up and still she wasn't building any value or getting any closer to owning a car.

4.4 Reliability, Used Cars, and Contingency Planning

A good used car is one of the excellent values available to consumers today—but isn't a new car more reliable than a used car? And don't teachers need a lot of reliability? The fact is that automotive technology has made the 2- and 3-year-old used cars of today far more reliable than the new cars of 10 years ago. Properly maintained, a car has a low probability of the kind of failure that will leave you on the side of the road and needing to get to school in a hurry. More likely is a nagging problem (like a "check engine" light) that needs to be addressed sometime but doesn't stop you in your tracks. Of course, anyone can have a flat tire, but that depends on the age of the tire and not the age of the car.

You may have heard that a new car loses a large portion of its value the moment it is driven off the dealer's lot. It's true—the car can no longer be sold as "new" and that makes a big difference. If you buy or lease a new car, you're on the losing end of that transaction. A used car buyer gets the benefit of the lower purchase price, even as the great majority of the car's useful life is still ahead.

Today there are many ways of coping with a car that needs repair, some of them new. Uber and Lyft are just two examples. Ride sharing services are expensive to use in the short term, but it's far more expensive if you get stampeded into a premature deal on a new car.

4.5 Shopping and Buying: Two Principles

The two best things you can do in car shopping are to (1) Keep it simple and (2) Keep it slow. Complexity and speed are your enemies. Let's see how these principles work out.

You can save thousands of dollars by keeping a car transaction simple—just buying a car. You will usually be far worse off if the transaction is a multi-part deal that involves trading in an old car, buying the next car, financing it and insuring it at the dealership. Let's take those parts one at a time:

- *Trading in an old car.* This won't be an issue for a first-time buyer but others will face it. When you trade an old car on a new one, the value you're quoted becomes part of the deal. Even people who are good with numbers can, in the moment, make a bad deal. It may sound nice to hear you're getting a great price for your trade, but if you are, that's because the dealer is willing to come down on the price of the new car. Often the straight-up price is better than the trade deal that's offered—but, more importantly, adding the trade to the transaction makes it harder to know whether you're getting a good deal.
- *Buying the next car.* If you focus on this you will not be distracted by the other parts of the deal.
- *Financing the car.* This step is often part of the negotiation and it can be dangerous to you as a buyer. Sales reps have been known to pretend they're coming down on the price of a car when actually they're coming up with different financing terms. Outright lying is rare but mistaken impressions are common.
- *Insuring the car.* Naturally you'll need to have legal insurance under your state's laws. A separate transaction is the best way to handle this. But the dealership will also offer insurance against unexpected repairs (extended warranties). Among automotive insiders these are known as bad deals almost all of the time. If you're making a lot of decisions at once they're likely to be bad. With time to consider and good information, many people would refuse extended warranties. But when these same people are at the dealership buying a car, they often experience a desire to "get it over with" by signing up for an extended warranty.

All of this argues for keeping it simple, but why keep it slow? It's because automotive deals seldom get worse with time but often get better. It takes time to do your homework by arranging financing and checking on insurance before going car shopping. It will take extra time if you sell your old car yourself or collect several different offers on it before going shopping, but that time will be well rewarded with a better deal.

4.6   Terry's Problem

In our opening case study, part of Terry's problem was not making a smart choice in choosing a car (luxury sport-utility instead of something more modest). Another big part of the problem was in executing the purchase and the lease. Here's how it happened: Terry went to the dealership without a strong feeling about what to buy but knowing a payment of about $350 per month would be affordable.

After a test drive (and yes, the sales rep did say, "You look great in this car") it was deal-making time. The sales rep first worked out a purchase price and loan agreement for 48 months, and apologetically looked up from the computer screen to say that, for 48 months, the payment would be $870 per month. Terry went into sticker shock but did remember to say the words memorized from an online article: "That's not good enough." The sales rep said, "I think we can get that down" and came back with a monthly payment of $598. But the loan period had been extended to 72 months and the sales rep didn't exactly stress that fact to Terry. Again from Terry: "That's not good enough," followed by the question, "Well, what monthly payment could you afford?" When Terry said, "$350," she was on her way to a truly bad choice. The sales rep said, "I don't think we can get there but we do have some special lease incentives. Let me go talk to my manager."

The sales rep returned with a handshake for emotional commitment and said, "You're going to have this car for under $350 a month!" Terry signed the lease paperwork and drove home that night in a brand-new luxury sport utility vehicle—affordable on a teacher's salary.

Terry made a big but understandable mistake by negotiating on the monthly car payment. Terry thought bargaining about the actual price of the car was going on as the monthly payments got lower. In fact there were no discounts at all. The successively lower payments offered by the sales rep were simply financing variations. Terry went away feeling like a winner, having paid thousands more than a good bargainer would have paid, and started down the road of always leasing and never owning a car.

4.7   Teachers and Negotiating

Suppose you thought about having a car sales rep come in and handle your classes one day. That's a weird thought experiment, but let's follow it a minute. You would provide some lesson plans, the car sales rep would take your classes, and again in a few years the car sales rep might try it again. Do you think that this unconventional substitute teacher would do a good job with your classes? No, of course not.

But to turn it around: When you go into a car dealership just once in 5 or 10 years, negotiating against someone who does it every day, do you think you'll get a good deal? No, of course not. So how can a teacher with little experience in negotiating drive away with a good deal? The first step is to realize you almost certainly won't do a good job negotiating against a pro, any more than a car sales rep would do a good job in your classroom.

Concentrate instead on the advantages you do have. You have access to a great deal of high-quality information because of the Internet and you probably have good information-seeking skills because of your profession. You can get a great deal (or avoid the worst deals) using the following strategies:

4.7.1 Negotiating Strategies

- **Consider not negotiating at all**. So-called "one-price" outlets like CarMax state the final sales price up front and claim not to negotiate any reductions. If you offer $1 less than the asking price it's no deal. These prices are pre-discounted to about what a negotiated deal would be. Although this will rarely be the best deal, you should make sure not to pay more than this price at the end of a negotiated deal elsewhere.
- **Check out discount plans**. If you are member of a road club like AAA, a warehouse club like Costco, or even a local credit union, you may be able to buy through a discount plan that, again, does not put your negotiating skills to the test.
- **Resist time pressure**. When a car dealer tells you that you have to make a decision right away, that's most often not strictly true. Time is on your side and haste works against you.
- **Don't fall in love with a car**. An old proverb says, "Never fall in love with anything that can't love you back." (A car can't.) Notice that the old proverb doesn't says "never fall in love with anything that *doesn't* love you back." Romantic interests can always change, but a car can never love you. If you have to have a particular car, you're likely to get a bad deal.
- **Negotiate up from cost rather than down from list**. At sites like Edmunds (edmunds.com), Kelly Blue Book (kbb.com), and Consumer Reports (consumerreports.org, with membership) you can get good information on dealer costs. Psychologically, you're likely to get a better deal starting with cost and adding money for the dealer, as opposed to starting at list and coming down—even coming down what seems like a large amount.

Among car dealers there is a saying that 80% of the profit comes from 20% of the customers. As a teacher, you don't want to be in that 20%—leave that for people with more money and more vanity than you.

4.7.2   The Dangers of Long Loans

During a car shopping session, a long loan can seem to solve your affordability problem. It makes the payments lower. You may feel that you'll always have a car payment anyway. But long car loans have a number of drawbacks.

With a long loan you're likely to owe more on the car than it is worth. That's known as being "upside down." If you own a car worth $12,000 but you owe $14,000 on it, you are vulnerable. Should the car become a total loss ("get totaled") in an accident, you owe the finance company $14,000 and not $12,000. Even when your car insurance covers the $12,000, you have to come up with $2000 somehow. Being upside down is common with long loans.

With a long loan you're more likely to buy "too much car." As an educator, it's essential for you to get to school and back and as a consumer you want a nice car. But as we have seen, modest cars will meet your transportation requirements. The additional money you spend because of a long loan is likely to go to options, accessories, or luxury upgrades whose cost is disguised when spread out over the life of the loan.

With a long loan, you're statistically more likely to default. You pay more interest over the life of the loan, you're upside down longer and more things can go wrong. Default and repossession are traumatic and worth a lot of trouble to avoid.

With a long loan, you're delaying the time that you can use cash each month to build your wealth. Paying off a car is a great feeling. It is achievable, and not just by the wealthy.

4.8   Car Maintenance

It's easy to advise people to do all of the recommended service in the owner's manual on time. That's not a bad idea and you will get longer life out of a car if you do. You can still get good results, though, with less than perfect maintenance. Cars are built today to go a lot longer without service. A minimal service plan would call for getting the oil changed on schedule and keeping all safety items up to date, and then fixing other things as they break. Somewhere between "doing everything" and this minimal service plan you'll probably find the best service plan for you.

Although some people think that always getting the recommended service at the authorized dealer is a good strategy, you have to pay attention. Some dealerships have been known to bundle in extra unneeded service at regular intervals, so that if you say "Just do the 60,000 mile service," you may get more than the manufacturer recommends. You should also be aware that in regular consumer surveys, auto repair satisfaction tends to be higher for independent garages than for car dealerships.

4.9   The Endgame: When to Let It Go

Although cars are durable and reliable for many miles, every car comes to the point at which it's smart to consider letting it go. Just as in buying a car, it's important to make this decision (1) with good information and (2) not in a hurry. "Good information" means getting a good idea of what your car is worth from sources like Edmunds (edmunds.com) and Kelly Blue Book (kbb.com) and finding a good price for your repair. Shopping around for repair quotes is hard if a car won't move, but in many cases an oncoming major repair gives early warning. "Not in a hurry" is a vitally important part of your strategy. Above all, don't get stampeded into buying a new car on unfavorable terms because you need something right away. Almost everybody has a way to get around temporarily while making a decision on repairing a car. It may seem expensive to take Uber or Lyft to work, or inconvenient to ask around for rides, but you can lose a lot of money on fast car decisions.

There is no mathematical formula that can tell you when to let a car go. Ideally, if you could know what the car was worth unrepaired and then with repairs fully done, you could subtract to find out whether the repair was worthwhile. A broken $6000 car that requires a $3000 engine job—and is then worth $10,000 fixed—is easily worth keeping. But it's hard to know what the car is truly worth in its unrepaired state.

Although there's no formula for a case like this, there are some rough guidelines. If a repair will cost more than half of the car's as-is value, or more than a few months' payments on a new car, it may not be worth fixing. But a car with a good exterior and interior and a previously good track record can be worth spending a substantial sum of money for a rebuilt engine or transmission.

These are difficult decisions sometimes, but it's important to be honest with yourself. Don't say "My old car died so I had to buy a new one," if "died" means that the battery failed.

4.10   Conclusion: Teachers and Cars

The natural empathy, openness and conscientiousness of teachers can put you at a disadvantage when it comes to car deals in general. You empathize with a sales rep who pretends to be taking a big personal loss on the favorable deal you're being offered. You're open about what you can afford and that can be used against you. You're conscientious about being at school where you're needed, and you don't want a car breakdown ever to get in the way. Yet with good decision-making, keeping things simple and keeping things slow, you can have great transportation on your way to building a secure future.

4.11   Teacher Tipsheet on Cars and Transportation

* Think about your transportation requirements and work to satisfy those instead of falling in love with a car.
* Keep your car transactions simple. Complexity is your enemy and you will get worse results with a combined purchase, trade of old car, financing, and insurance deal.
* Keep your car transactions slow. Speed is your enemy and you should do whatever it takes to avoid being rushed into a deal.
* Take advantage of the abundant information available when you are buying a car and do not assume you are a good negotiator.
* Maintain your car properly and be smart when an old car needs major repairs.
* Do not assume you'll always be making a loan or lease payment and understand the advantages of paying off a car to build wealth.

4.12   Q&A

1. Are you saying teachers should drive clunkers?
   – No! A properly maintained car will not look like a clunker. Look around the parking lot at school and you'll see a variety of ages of cars. Keep in mind that a 10- or even 15-year old used car can look fine even if its style is obviously dated. Also keep in mind that as you build financial security over the years, you can drive what you like. We're mostly against buying

"too much car" too soon in a teaching career and getting behind on financial goals as a result.

2. All of my friends have car payments and think they will forever. Why shouldn't I?
   - When you understand the power of paying off a car, and then continuing to make payments to yourself, we think you'll agree with us that this is a good move. Keep in mind that if you're like most teachers, your community and professional peers are not the sort to be easily impressed by a new or stylish car. It's certainly not worth incurring a lot of debt.

3. Aren't the "one-price" car dealers like CarMax fairly expensive? Can't I beat their deals?
   - Yes, they are fairly expensive. They preset their prices *not* at the level a really good negotiator would achieve, but somewhat higher than that, though below the worst deals. Very few dealerships will fail to at least match a price from a "one-price" dealer. Be careful, though, to compare apples to apples. If a "one-price" dealer has a hassle-free 7-day trial ownership period and you value that, the car is worth more than a very similar one down the street without a trial ownership period.

4.13   Financial 911 for Teachers

You're have a financial 911 when your car is in danger of being repossessed. This will happen if you're so far behind on your payment that the lender may take the car back and sell it. If the sale brings in more than the remaining loan balance you receive a check for the difference. More often, the sale price is less than your loan balance. You owe the difference and the lender may come after you to get that amount. Here are some facts to know about repossession:

- In an "involuntary repossession," the lender hires someone to come and get the car. In most states this can happen without notice. You just go out to drive to school one morning and your car is gone.
- Lenders are not diligent about getting the best price for a repossessed car, often just selling it for what it will bring at a wholesale auction. You are also charged fees for the repossession and storage, further reducing your chances of breaking even on the deal.
- In a "voluntary repossession" you return the car and declare that you're giving it up. This is not good but it's better than involuntary repossession because you get to plan what to do next and your fees are lower.

If you're behind on your car payments and feel involuntary repossession is possible, it's better to do a voluntary repossession and find a way, any way, to get to your job for the time being. It may hurt your pride, but you have friends or coworkers or family who would want to help out. The worst outcome is to remain in denial and find your car repossessed, so be realistic about that possibility.

It's easy to say "Don't borrow so much," because excessive borrowing in the past is often the source of your car problem. But when you're facing repossession you can't focus on the past. Concentrate on not making your car loan problem any worse. Check into low cost options (including a clunker that will at least get you back and forth to work) and be careful not to make things worse with a truly bad car deal.

5

Walls and a Roof: Housing for Teachers

5.1 Teacher Case Study: Too Good to Be True?

Clayton and Katrina had both been brought up with the saying, "If it sounds too good to be true, it probably is." They stared at the mortgage refinancing quote, ran the numbers again, and took the leap. And it turned out as well as they had hoped, or better.

Clayton and Katrina, both teachers, had bought a nice but modest house. The $1140 monthly payment was a stretch at first. Still, as they moved up the pay scale it became affordable. Fifteen years later, they had paid the original $225,000 balance down to $146,000—a huge remaining sum to them. By refinancing, they would have a payment of $1009 a month and still pay off the house in 2033 (a year that sounded far away, like science fiction, when they had bought).

The number that looked too good to be true was the monthly payment – $130 less per month. Was it too good to be true? No, as it turned out. They took half of their monthly savings, $65, and Clayton and Katrina used that for a monthly "date night," as they heard recommended in an enrichment class. Over time they came to call it "refinance date night" and it became a family story. The other $65 they put into a long-term account for their future. Over the 15 years of the refinanced loan, that account grew to $20,000.

Date night monthly for 15 years and $20,000 more in long-term savings! And all they had to do was fill out some paperwork and go to a loan office. It had sounded too good to be true, but it was real – every bit of it.

T. Hunt Ferrarini et al., *Teachers Can Be Financially Fit*,
https://doi.org/10.1007/978-3-030-49356-1_5

5.2   A Roof Over Your Head: Rent or Buy?

Paying for a place to live will be the single largest monthly expense in most teachers' budgets. To get ahead you will need to manage this carefully. Everybody needs shelter, but beyond that there are a lot of decisions to be made. One of the first is whether to rent or buy.

5.2.1   Advantages of Buying

For most teachers, buying a home will be a good long-run strategy. Home ownership comes with a number of advantages:

- It is a place all your own, so you have greater privacy and more control than with typical rentals.
- Your housing costs are more stable and predictable because you're usually paying with a fixed-rate mortgage that gives you the same payment each month.
- You have greater ties to your community. This can be a special advantage if you teach in the same school district where you live. Research suggests that teachers do not move long distances or across state lines as frequently as other career professionals, and so "settling down" may be more feasible for you.
- Financially, the home operates as a tax-advantaged investment plan of sorts. The house will typically grow in value and you will also pay down the loan over time, making the house a source of wealth. (The value of the house minus what you owe is referred to as "equity.")

5.2.2   Advantages of Renting

Other teachers will decide that homeownership is not the best option right away, or ever. Renting will give you these advantages:

- You're not committed to live in a particular place, and that is especially important if you think you may be moving to a new school district soon.
- You do not have to come up with a lot of money to rent a new place, as opposed to a home purchase, which requires thousands of dollars for a down payment and closing costs.

- Unlike a homeowner, you are not responsible for paying for repairs. The landlord is responsible for those.
- Although you do not get the tax-advantaged investment of home ownership, you also do not face the risk of losing money on a house when you sell.

All things considered, a good rule for teachers is not to buy a house unless you expect to stay in an area for at least 5 years. That will give you time to recover from move-in costs and let the house appreciate in value. For shorter time periods it is usually better to rent.

If you have a goal of home ownership and are currently renting, you may have heard the saying that your rent money is "wasted" or "down the drain." That's not strictly true since you are paying rent money in exchange for a place to live and the amount you pay is often less than buying. It's a good strategy to continue to rent while saving money and checking out areas and possibilities for your new home. Buying a home too soon can lead to many more problems than continuing to rent for a time.

5.3 How Much Can You Afford (Should You Stretch)?

The decision to buy depends partly on what you could afford—why bother if what you can afford to buy isn't nearly as nice as what you could rent? To get a general idea, multiply your household's before-tax annual income by 2 or 2.5. That's the price of home you could typically afford.

Clayton and Katrina in our opening case study, like typical pairs of teachers nationally, can afford modest houses. With national average starting salaries at about $40,000 for teachers (times 2 or 2.5), their purchase price could be around $160,000 to $200,000. A purchase price of around $200,000 is near the median in most areas of the country.

Before you get serious about house-hunting, you would want to make more detailed calculations taking into account your household debt situation, credit score, and other factors. Search *housing affordability calculator* and you'll find good estimating tools. Nothing says you will have an easy time financially, but homeownership will be feasible.

The situation is different in some high cost-of-living areas. There the solutions are not as easy:

- You can defer homeownership much longer by renting and building your financial resources.
- You can take in a roommate, as permitted by lease agreements and regulation. This can be a great solution for both of you if you have compatible tastes and lifestyles, and a nightmare otherwise.
- You can buy a home in a more affordable area with a longer commute.
- You can move to a teaching job in lower-cost area.

Whether you live in a high-cost or low-cost area, housing is a fixed cost in your budget. You have to come up with the money every month. In just about every house hunt, people think about "stretching" a little beyond what's comfortable to pay. What are the arguments for doing that?

1. Your pay will go up over time, making your new home more affordable.
   - Using the standard rule, a pair of teachers earning $60,000 each at mid-career could afford a house of around $240,000 to $300,000. That's going to be a much nicer house than the $160,000 to $200,000 house affordable to starting teachers. So why not just stretch to $240,000 or a little beyond for that first house?
   - It is a reasonable gamble to assume that your pay will increase over time, but a gamble all the same. If you have stretched to buy a nicer house, the greatest danger will be shortly after you move in. At this point you are vulnerable to financial setbacks when you can least afford them. Still, if you are a public school teacher you do have the advantage of being unlikely to be laid off in an economic downturn.
2. Your home is an investment.
   - To an extent this point is true. You're not just paying for housing—you're also putting money aside in an asset that may grow over time. But like any investment, a house may go up or down in value. In the 2008 financial crisis, housing prices dropped 19% nationally—only to rocket past their former peak with a 27% rise that started in 2012. Volatile markets such as Arizona suffered larger losses and greater gains.
   - If you have stretched to buy a nicer house, you may find yourself house-rich and cash-poor. You could show a nice value for the home on your household financial statement but would not be able to use that value to pay bills. You could tap some of that value with a home equity loan but that would raise a lot of additional issues, explored later in this chapter.
3. It's for the family.
   - Emotions can run high when you are house-hunting. Still, it is important to be realistic about what your family will enjoy. More room and a

cozy fireplace are great, but not if there is constant stress about how to meet the monthly payment. Before you spend a lot of housing money on behalf of your children, get realistic. Kids are surprisingly unaware of the finer details of their housing. Even the supposed necessity of having one bedroom per child can get in the way of good housing decisions. "One room per child" does not prepare kids for the time that they will need to share quarters with others, such as when they go to college or into volunteer or military service. "One room per child" is nice, but it's not a necessity, as the experience of many societies over places and times (most likely including your own family's past) reveals.

5.4   The "Happy-o-Stat" Applied to Housing: Location, Location, and Location

You'll recall the "happy-o-stat," our name for the way a new purchase becomes routine after a while and then provides less satisfaction. The "happy-o-stat" applies to housing, but not in the same way to every nice feature of a house.

Housing features such as fireplaces and even a swimming pool can become routine over time. They can require more maintenance and be used less often than a house-hunter would think. Stretching to a higher payment to get a fireplace or pool may not be a good use of money.

Research indicates, however, that the happiness of relatively short commutes and the unhappiness of long commutes are highly durable. There are also continuing benefits of being in a good neighborhood and in the same school district where you are employed. If you're going to stretch, then stretching to get a good location makes sense.

Real estate agents are fond of telling customers that the three most important attributes of any property are "location, location, and location." As with most such humorous sayings, there's an element of truth. You can add a fireplace or swimming pool in the future if you have a good location, but you can't add a good location to a house that lacks it.

With all this in mind, you may want to move at some point, leaving behind a perfectly good house that's just in the wrong place. Or you may move because of a distant opportunity. Moving is a lot of work but it can greatly improve your job prospects and it does not have to be expensive. If you do decide to move, check on moving container options that let you pack a large container on your own time. When you're done the operator delivers that container to your new home, where you do the unpacking. Such a move can be much less expensive than a full-service pack-and-move by a traditional mover.

5.5 Mortgage Loans

Since very few are able to pay cash for a house, you will probably be borrowing money. It will likely be the largest loan transaction you will ever make. A key part of your housing strategy is therefore your loan strategy. You have two big decisions to make: the size of the down payment and the length of the loan.

5.5.1 Size of the Down Payment

There are important advantages to making a down payment of 20% or more. To begin with, your monthly payment is less. And in the early years of ownership you are much less likely to be "upside down" on the house (owing more than the house is worth). Only in a major crisis do home prices fall more than 20%.

If you go for a down payment under 20%, you might be required to pay for private mortgage insurance. PMI protects the lender if you default on the loan. When you pay it, it's just a fee and it's not going toward principal and interest. You're getting more for your money if you have started with at least 20% down.

The downside of a big down payment is obvious—it's hard to come up with that kind of cash. Therefore it's attractive, especially to first-time home-buyers, to go for a smaller down payment just to get into a house and get started on homeownership.

5.5.2 Length of the Loan

The second big decision to make is the length of the loan. There are important advantages to a 15-year loan. The interest savings run to many thousands of dollars because you are not borrowing money for so long. A 30-year-loan is much more common because the monthly payments are lower, even if the overall interest expense is so much more. Be aware that in the early years of a 30-year loan, your payments will be mostly interest to the lender. You are paying down the loan balance very slowly. The standing joke in the early years of the loan is that you're not a homeowner, but a "mailbox owner." The lender still owns the rest. That's not literally true (You own the house, but it's secured by the lender's ability to throw you out if you don't pay.) Still, the slow payoff of the balance is real.

5.5.3 Deciding on the Mortgage Loan

You may see the advice to buy only the house you can afford with a 15-year mortgage, a 20% down payment, and a monthly payment only as high as a fourth of your take-home pay. That is highly restrictive advice and it would limit you to the least expensive houses starting out. If you have relative job security, as most public school teachers do, a 30-year mortgage will be fine if the monthly payment takes no more than 28% of your gross income (assuming your other debts are under control).

Do not assume that your monthly house payment will be comfortable just because a lender has approved you for the loan. Experience shows that some lenders are willing to go along if you're stretching hard to afford a house. Experience also shows that some lenders are willing to put you into exotic mortgage alternatives that are not nearly as simple as standard 15- and 30-year mortgages. We recommend that teachers generally avoid these options because of their increased risk. The options include adjustable rate mortgages, balloon mortgages, and interest-only loans. The one thing they all have in common is the possibility that you will face much higher payments at some point. That risk is absent in 15- and 30-year fixed-rate mortgages.

5.6 House-Hunting, Start to Finish

What are the actual steps in the biggest and most complicated transaction you're likely ever to make? Here's how it happens:

1. You do some window-shopping and dreaming. Before you do anything formal, you get to know the area. Having this time is a major advantage of renting first in the general area where you want to buy. Sites such as Zillow.com and Trulia.com are great for finding out about neighborhoods and homes. Still, there are things about an area that you just can't find out online or in a hurry.
2. You get pre-qualified for a loan by taking your financial records to apply with a lender. Although the pre-qualification is not a definite commitment by the lender, it's an excellent indication of how much money you can borrow.

3. You hunt houses. At some point in this stage you will usually become involved with a real estate agent. Arrangements are a little different in every state, but most of the time—you should understand—the real estate agent you're working with is not "your agent." Instead, both the listing agent and the agent you're working with are paid by the seller (usually a fixed percentage of the sale price).

4. You make an offer. Unlike a casual car offer at a dealership, the real estate offer is serious business. The offer is a multi-page contract specifying the price you're proposing to pay and a lot of conditions on the offer. Typical conditions (or "contingencies") include:

   - Home inspection. A thorough going-over by a qualified inspector will typically be required by your lender. Your home offer will say what happens if major flaws are found during inspection. Sometimes the problems are so extensive that the deal is cancelled. More often there will be repairs, allocated as agreed between buyer and seller.
   - A loan contingency. This says that if you, the buyer, don't get financing the deal is off. Remember that although you may be pre-approved, financing isn't final until contracts are signed on the particular property and terms of your transaction.
   - An appraisal. The lender will want an expert to estimate the fair market value of the home, using experience and local comparable transactions. If this estimate is at or above what you're offering to pay, fine. If the appraisal comes in low, adjustments may be necessary. Remember that the lender's interests are protected by the value of the home, so a good appraisal is necessary for the lender to take the risk. Your offer is accompanied by "earnest money," an amount that shows you are serious about offering to buy the property. The amount can range from $500 on up to 3% or more of the offering price. (This is quite unlike a car deal, in which it doesn't cost you anything to say, "I'll offer you $28,500 for that car.") If your offer is turned down by the seller, you get the earnest money back. If the offer goes through, it's built into the deal as part of your down payment. But if your offer is accepted and you back out, you lose the earnest money. That's why it's important only to make a formal offer if you're seriously interested in a property.

5. You negotiate toward a completed sales contract. On rare occasions your first offer is accepted and you take the next steps. More likely, the seller will ask for more than you are offering. You may accept that offer or make your own counteroffer, which in turn may be accepted or rejected. Keep in

mind that just about everything is up for negotiation. If the seller wants to take the appliances but you'd prefer that they remain, offers go back and forth.

This is a good time to remember that, unless you specifically signed a contract to be represented by a "buyer's agent," your real estate agent is not really your agent. Most agents are ethical and will not go against your interests—but then again, most will not be completely aggressive in trying to get the lowest price for you. Remember that "your" agent only gets paid if the deal goes through, so above all that agent has reasons to move the transaction forward. At some point, you either don't have a deal or you do. If you do, then both parties sign the sales contract as amended in your negotiations.

Despite the increased stakes, most people are less likely to get a bad deal in real estate than in cars. It is easy to overpay for a car in negotiations with a dealer, but harder to overpay for a house because of the lender's involvement. Most real estate decisions give you a matter of days rather than the hours or minutes of a car transaction.

6. Now the inspection goes forward and you formally apply for the loan with final sales contract in hand. Snags and delays are possible at any point. All of the contingencies must be satisfied. If the inspection finds deficiencies, you deal with them as specified in the contract. Sometimes additional negotiations become necessary. The lender puts together a complete package of papers necessary to lend you the money and secure its interests.

7. When all of the contingencies have been satisfied and financing has been approved, it's time to set a closing, a legal meeting in which you sign over the money and formally take possession. If the transaction is unusual in any way, you are best served by having a real estate attorney represent you. In ways that first-time homebuyers may not be aware of, a real estate transaction is extremely complicated. Anything from an incorrect lot boundary to an unpaid tax bill can derail the closing. The attorney is there to see that your interests are protected. If your transaction is routine, however, the closing may be handled by a "settlement agent" who is not an attorney.

5.7   After You Move In

House-hunting and negotiating and going to closing can be exciting. Actually living in the house is another matter. The two main things to remember are maintenance and refinancing.

Now that you're a homeowner, the responsibility for maintenance is entirely yours. Experienced homeowners can tell that there's always something that needs fixing. Therefore perfect maintenance is not a realistic goal. What is important is paying special attention to items that have large future costs if neglected. A leaking roof is a good example. If you there are wet places in the ceiling indicating that water is getting in somehow, quick action is necessary. In the early stages, it may be nothing more than a bad seal around a vent pipe or chimney. If neglected, leakage can cause expensive structural problems. Water leakage is in a different category from faded exterior trim or other cosmetic problems that can wait.

Now that you have a long fixed-rate mortgage, you're in a fortunate position something like "Heads I win, tails you lose" on interest rates. Interest rates on home mortgages can change significantly, both up and down. When interest rates go up you don't have to pay more. You keep your same monthly payment. But when they go down you can get a lower payment by refinancing. This means that you take out a new loan to cover the remaining balance and enjoy the monthly savings.

When do you consider refinancing? One rule of thumb is to think about it when interest rates have dropped more than 2 percentage points. Another rule of thumb says you should refinance when your lower monthly payments would pay off the costs of refinancing within 2 years. All of this assumes, of course, that you're staying in the house. If you are getting ready to move, you don't refinance since you won't remain in the house long enough to recoup the costs.

5.8   Avoiding Refinancing Traps

Refinancing is a powerful technique for wealth building but it can go badly if you're not careful. In our opening teacher case study, Clayton and Katrina used refinancing to increase their wealth and quality of life. As important as "what they did" is "what they didn't do":

- They didn't get a "cash out" refinancing in which the new payments come with a lump sum of money to spend. That would amount to spending down their home equity—understandable in an emergency but a terrible idea for financing a vacation.
- They didn't refinance their 30-year loan for another 30 years, thereby extending their payoff date another 15 years into the future. Instead they refinanced for 15 years, getting a lower interest rate and keeping their original payoff date.

- They didn't buy that first home without paying attention to the long term. The neighborhood and the home were sound, so when it turned out they liked their jobs they were able to stay in the house and keep paying down the mortgage. Of course, they were free to move at any time. The quality of the home would have made for a relatively easy sale as they moved on or moved up.
- They didn't just blow the savings of refinancing. They could have done anything with that money. If they had been focused on maximizing their wealth, they could have invested it all. They ended up investing half and spending half. If they had gone without an intentional plan about the savings, the money likely would all have been spent.
- They didn't refinance using a lender who hunted them down. They understood that actively checking conventional online and local lenders was the best way to go, rather than accepting a telemarketed deal that showed up on the phone one day. (So-called "predatory lenders" abound in refinancing, peddling bad deals, often with cash back and unusually high rates.)

5.9 When You Sell

The first step in a good home sale is having made smart decisions when buying. If you did your homework then, you did not overpay or buy into a declining neighborhood. But however good or bad your decisions were, at selling time there are two main things to remember: (1) Don't sell in a hurry; and (2) Be intentional about working with a real estate agent.

If you sell in a hurry, you're likely to lose thousands of dollars of value. A proper sale requires time to get the house and surroundings looking great. It also requires patience, as real estate sales proceed on a slower time scale than other things you might sell. Therefore it often pays to do what it takes to avoid a forced quick sale (for example, changing the timing of a move or renting instead of immediately buying in a new area).

Almost always you will want to work with a real estate agent in selling. The commissions will cost you thousands of dollars but a good real estate agent is worth it. A good agent will not overprice your home, so you won't have to go long weeks or months and then lower the price, realizing it was too high to begin with. Equally well, a good agent will not underprice your home, leaving you to wonder whether it could have sold for much more. Teachers are especially vulnerable to bad real estate representation because there are so many low-volume agents who are former teachers. If you ask around, you'll find that the most active agents tend to be the best. This is no time for loyalty to a retired teacher who used to work at your school and now does a little real estate on the side.

Sometimes you may feel confident enough to offer your house "For Sale by Owner." If you truly know what you're doing you can save thousands. You can also lose thousands because of your inexperience in a highly complicated transaction. "You don't know what you don't know" – that is, there will be traps that you don't even know to think about unless you have a great deal of experience.

5.10   Conclusion: Teachers and Housing

On a teacher's pay you cannot afford to make big housing mistakes. If you do your homework and remain patient, you will do fine. On a teacher's pay you'll be near the middle of the housing market. Most likely, you did not get into teaching because you expected an affluent lifestyle. With smart decisions, you can be living in medium quality housing with a higher than average quality of life because of your satisfying career choice.

5.11   Teacher Tipsheet on Housing

- Carefully consider when you should rent as opposed to buying a home.
- There are good reasons to "stretch" a little to pay for a bigger or nicer house but be careful not to get over-extended.
- There are many tradeoffs in housing decisions. Think carefully before locking yourself into a long commute to school in return for better housing.
- Stick with conventional fixed-rate mortgages.
- House-hunting is not quick or easy but you'll do fine if you know and follow the steps.
- After moving in, maintain your home properly even if you can't maintain it perfectly.
- Refinancing can be a real wealth builder if you do it properly.
- When you sell a house, you'll be helped by your original smart decisions in buying and by working with a good real estate agent.

5.12   Q&A

1. Why should we teachers settle for less in housing than other professionals?
   - The short answer is that we make less money than other professionals. If we count doctors and business executives as our peer group, we will always have trouble matching their lifestyles. Keeping up with their housing will often involve over-borrowing and a lack of "wiggle room" in the rest of our budgets. This is a good time to remember that teachers' careers have a high component of "psychic income" – the good feeling we have from doing a vital and satisfying job. Unlike money income, psychic income cannot be spent to get more material goods, but it can leave us happier.

2. Is a home equity loan or line of credit a good idea?
   - Usually not. Building equity in a house is an important way of becoming wealthier over time. Borrowing against that equity slows down the process. As a later chapter shows in detail, borrowing to purchase anything with a short useful life is a bad idea. Most things you would buy with a home equity loan or line of credit will have a shorter useful life than the time you'll take to pay back the loan – leaving you at some point with more debt and nothing to show for it.

3. Why should I pay thousands of dollars to a real estate agent when I sell?
   - A good agent will produce thousands of dollars in value for you. That agent will shepherd you through the selling process, making sure that your home is priced right and marketed well. During negotiations, the agent will be a buffer between you and your buyers so that you can take your time to evaluate offers. When complications come up, the agent will operate as a "fixer" to see that they are taken care of. Equally true, a bad agent is not worth the thousands, and will simply stand by to collect commission dollars. That is why it is so important to choose an agent carefully.

5.13   Financial 911 for Teachers

You have a financial 911 when you are in danger of foreclosure or homelessness. Both are serious, but homelessness is among the worst crises anyone could face.

Foreclosure will happen if you get too far behind on your house payments. The papers signed at the time of purchase give the lender the right to evict you and sell the house to recover some or all of the loan balance. Here are some facts to know about foreclosure:

- Lenders do not quickly or casually foreclose. They would prefer that you remain in the home and catch up on your payments. Therefore foreclosure will not happen without multiple warnings that give you a chance to catch up and avoid eviction.
- Avoiding the lender is not a good strategy when you are behind on house payments. Lenders understand that events such as layoffs, divorces, or serious medical problems can cause people to be late with house payments. They will typically work with you if you contact them early on. Personal relationships can be important and you cannot have a good relationship with a lender you are avoiding.
- If you owe more on a house than it is worth, your lender may agree to a "short sale." In a short sale, the lender agrees to accept the amount yielded by the sale as payment for the loan. Thus the lender is taking a loss. The lender won't be happy about this but may well prefer it to foreclosure and eviction.
- If you even think you might get close to foreclosure, you need to put yourself on a strict budget and marshal all of your financial resources. In the most recent financial crisis there were homes that went to foreclosure even as the owners continued luxuries such as premium cable entertainment packages and club memberships.

Even worse than a looming foreclosure is sudden homelessness. Most teachers do not think about ever being homeless themselves, but it happens. This is not the outcome of a usual spending pattern, but more often the result of domestic situations, addictions, or similar traumas. If you soon will not have anywhere to stay, this is a true financial 911 and it calls for whatever is necessary to avoid homelessness.

In such a situation, do not let pride get in your way. Talk with family and friends and local service agencies – anyone who might be able to help you avoid being without shelter. It's important to plan out where you will go on the very first night you expect to be homeless. Do not count on just spending one night in your car before taking action. The objective is to avoid a downward spiral of bad decisions. Even the most logical among us will make terrible decisions after spending the night in a car, unable to take a shower before heading off to school.

6

Managing Credit and Debt

6.1 Teacher Case Study: The School Human Resources Department

An inner-city charter school, with a focus on business and finance, required all of their students to take classes in personal finance, economics, and business. Not surprisingly, this K-8 school was interested in hiring teachers with a strong background in these business-related areas.

The students, parents, administrators, and school board members were under the impression that their teachers were experts in personal financial literacy. How could they not be, when they teach at a school that specialized in training students in these areas at all grade levels? It turned out, however, to be a significant challenge to staff the school in this manner. Few teachers study these topics in their teacher preparation programs and this modest charter school's budget couldn't afford to pay the kinds of salaries required to attract teachers experienced in finance.

As is discussed in another chapter in this book, the teachers were constantly hearing about how important it is to prepare for their own retirements. Most everyone is aware that saving for the future is important, but at this school, the teachers were bombarded with financial information through the lessons they were expected to teach every day. A theme they constantly heard was that everyone in the building should be contributing to the school's 401(K) plan up to the amount the school was willing to match. Not to do so is throwing away free money the school is trying to give you. Put another way, such a decision is like saying "no thank you" to an instant 100% return.

T. Hunt Ferrarini et al., *Teachers Can Be Financially Fit*, https://doi.org/10.1007/978-3-030-49356-1_6

One day the school's Human Resources Director, Jose, was listening to a number of teachers provide lessons in which this same 401 (K) advice was being given to the students. He was alarmed because he knew confidentially that a large percentage of the teaching faculty at the school were having judgements deducted from their paychecks. Some of these were for past due childcare payments that a court had required be deducted for their earnings. However, the majority of the judgements were being sent to credit card companies, collection agencies, or even individual retail outlets. Anyone who gets into such a situation can find it difficult to also save for retirement and, equally importantly, their credit score is likely to be very poor which impacts them in all kinds of other places. Additionally, the resulting poor credit scores create multiple problems elsewhere. In theory, it is east to explain that everyone needs to be saving for their future; however, if you find yourself in debt with a low credit score it may be that this issue needs to addressed before you can move on to retirement planning.

6.2   Credit Matters

Credit allows individuals to obtain the use of money that they do not have. Obtaining credit, in practical terms, means convincing someone else (a lender) to provide a loan in return for a promise to pay it back, plus an additional charge called interest. Many people use credit, obtaining loans to buy cars, homes, and major appliances, to improve their homes, to pay for college education, and so forth. In our modern economy, it turns out that the credit scores assigned to each of us have a sizeable impact on our lives. Today these scores go beyond determining eligibility for loans. Credit scores can affect car insurance rates—and employers may even want to check your credit before a job offer is forthcoming, particularly if the job involves managing the firm's money.

Credit decisions can be difficult ones. Like all difficult decisions, they involve examining the advantages and disadvantages facing the individual making the choice. The hard part, of course, is figuring out if the advantages of using credit outweigh the disadvantages.

6.3   Is Credit from Heaven or Hell?

There are two important things to know about credit: it can work for you or it can work against you. The bright side of using credit is that it can help you acquire valuable assets – a home, for example, or an education. Assets are goods or services that typically retain or even increase in value. Credit can help you lead a happier life by allowing you to obtain the things you wish to have today but pay for them later. Credit can also help people in an emergency to pay for that unexpected vehicle repair or visit to the hospital.

There is also a dark side of using credit. Mistakes in using too much credit— in relation to your income—can be difficult to recover from. Increasingly, many new graduates from college or vocational schools spend a lot of the income they earn in their first jobs repaying large student loans and credit card debts they have racked up while in school. These repayments leave them less money to spend on current payments like an apartment, vehicle, food, and entertainment. Misusing credit—missing a payment or defaulting on a loan—can have many negative consequences including the inability to get credit later or having money deducted from your paycheck to be applied against delinquent loans.

6.4   Common Forms of Credit

Table 6.1 describes the conventional types of credit people use and the lenders that provide such credit. It also explains the advantages and disadvantages of various forms of credit. The table suggests a number of ways that credit can help people. For example, owing a home offers several advantages since homes frequently increase in value and the interest paid on these loans may be tax-deductible. Buying a home, however, represents a large, long-term, financial commitment and very few families could afford to purchase one without a home mortgage.

Credit card loans also offer advantages. They are convenient, easy to use, and often offer rewards. They can also be helpful in an emergency. And traveling without a credit card is difficult and inconvenient. But credit card loans can pose serious risks since they come with high interest rates and some people choose to borrow too much with them, given their level of income. When obtaining a new credit card, a little shopping around is a good idea. Credits cards differ in the interest rates and fees they charge as well as the kinds of rewards many allow you to earn. Other forms of credit also have advantages and disadvantages.

6.4.1   How Credit Works

Financial institutions (banks, savings and loan associations, credit unions, consumer finance companies) hold money that they are willing to lend. The owners of financial institutions, however, are not charities. They expect to be

Table 6.1   Forms of credit

Types of credit	Lender	Advantages	Disadvantages
Home mortgage	Commercial bank	Homes often increase in value.	Long-term commitments.
	Savings and loan	Interest rates are relatively low.	Involves an extensive credit check.
	Credit union	The interest paid is tax deductible.	
Car loans	Commercial bank	Cars provide an easy way to get to work and earn an income.	Cars lose a part of their value quickly upon purchase.
	Savings and loan		
	Credit union		
	Consumer finance company		
College loans	Commercial bank	A college education is typically a good investment.	Students sometimes borrow more than necessary.
	Savings and loan	Interest rates are frequently relatively low.	New graduates can face difficulty in repaying large loans.
	Credit union		
Personal loans	Commercial bank	Allow individuals to purchase something today and pay for it later.	Personal loans have relatively high interest rates.
	Savings and loan		Some young people may borrow more than they should at their level of income.
	Credit union		
	Consumer finance company		
Credit cards	Commercial bank	Credit cards are convenient to use and useful in an emergency.	Credit cards come with relatively high interest rates.
	Savings and loan	Credit card bills provide a record of charges and a way to dispute or stop faulty charges.	Some people may borrow more than they should at their level of income.
	Retail store	Some credit cards allow users to earn rewards.	
	Oil company		
	Consumer finance company		

compensated when they make a loan. This compensation is called interest. Interest is the price a borrower pays to a lender for use of the lender's deposits. Interest is the reward lenders receive for allowing others to use their deposits.

Both sides typically benefit in a credit transaction. Borrowers are able to purchase something that may be of value today and perhaps in the future. Lenders are repaid the money they loaned, plus interest. It can be a win-win deal for both parties—imagine a new college graduate with a great idea for a new business but without the funds to start the company. A bank may loan the money to start the firm in return for some interest for the use of their money over a period of time. In this case, both parties are pleased with the results of this deal.

An important factor in determining the rate of interest to be charged is the amount of confidence the lender has that the amount of the loan plus interest will be repaid in the agreed upon time. Higher risk loans—loans where it is uncertain that the borrower can repay—usually come with higher interest rates. Alternatively, lower risk loans typically come with lower interest rates.

Loans for something intangible (and unable to be seized if the borrower does not pay) like a vacation cost more in interest than for something tangible (and that can be seized by the borrower) like a home. When an asset is used to back a loan—like a home or car—this is said to be using collateral to obtain the loan.

6.4.2   How to Get Credit

To obtain credit, you need to contact a financial institution and complete a loan application. This can usually be taken care of online; however, you will also need to produce copies of other important financial documents too. Ordinarily, a loan application asks for at least the following information:

- Name
- Address (and recent addresses if you have moved recently)
- Employment record
- Other loans
- Credit card accounts
- Savings account
- Checking account
- Investment accounts

Since lenders are not operating charities, they are careful with their money. From their perspective, money has alternative uses. They could buy bonds, build a new building, invest in real estate, lend money to a small or a large business, or even hold the money for security purposes in their vault. As a result, it is typically stated that your access to credit depends on "the Three Cs of Credit":

- Character: Will the applicant be responsible and repay the money as agreed upon?
- Capacity: Does the applicant have enough income to comfortably make payments on the loan amount requested?
- Collateral: Will the loan be secured, or guaranteed, by collateral that can be used to repay the debt in case the borrower defaults on the loan?

6.5   Credit Reports and Scores

The primary way that a financial institution can make a judgement of your character and capacity for credit is to review your credit reports and credit scores. An important step toward obtaining credit at reasonable interest rates is building and maintaining a good credit history. A good credit history can make the difference between getting a loan or being turned down, or between paying high rate of interest or a low one. In addition, potential employers and landlords will often check an applicant's credit history before making a decision about offering a job or renting an apartment. Auto insurance companies may check your credit report to get an indication of your behavior, too.

6.5.1   What Is a Credit Report?

A credit report is a record of an individual's personal credit history. It is one good indicator of an applicant's character and whether he or she will repay borrowed money as agreed upon. A credit report will tell, in detail, how much the person has borrowed, from whom, and whether these bills have been paid on time. There are three agencies that issue credit reports:

- Equifax (800) 685–1111 or equifax.com
- Experian (888) 397–3742 or experian.com
- Trans Union (800) 888–4213 or transunion.com

Each credit report will include identifying information about you (Social Security number, address, date of birth, and so forth). It will include your credit history for all accounts with any creditors you have maintained. A list of credit inquiries will also be on the report including the agency that asked for your credit information. An inquiry will be generated each time you apply for credit or that you allow someone (like a landlord or employer) to check your credit reports. The report also includes any public record information including accounts in collection, bankruptcies, late payments, and so forth. And these reports are not static. Recently there has been talk of including cell phone payment and history and even information from a borrower's social media profile.

You will note that while credit reports include much information about you, they do not include everything. Nothing in your credit report speaks to your income, employment history, balances in your checking or savings accounts, other investments or assets, your race, religion, or other personal information.

6.5.2   Your Credit Score

Lastly, the credit reporting agencies translate your credit report into a credit score. This number is called your FICO score—named after the Fair Isaac Company that developed the most widely used scoring methodology. FICO scores range from 300 to 850. The higher the score the better. Each of the credit report agencies will produce a slightly different score for you based on small differences in their formulas.

Credit scores are weighted based on the various parts of your credit history:

- **Types of credit in use** counts for about 10% of the score.
- **New credit** counts for about 10%.
- **Length of credit history** counts for about 15%.
- **Amounts owed** counts for about 30%.
- **Payment history** accounts for about 25%.

You can see from this list that the most important factors in calculating your credit score are the amounts owed and your payment history. The amounts owed is generally calculated as a percentage of your total credit that you are using. For example, if you have three credit cards, each with a $1000 limit, and they are all at that limit your credit score will be lower. If you only have $100 charged on one of the three cards it will be much higher. Your payments history examines how well you have made the required payment (even if just the minimum) on your loans. Missing a payment, even if just for a month, can be damaging to your credit score. While the other three factors have a smaller effect, they are still important in maintaining a good credit score. If most of your loans are in secured loans like a car or home payment that is better for your credit score than having revolving, credit card-type loans. When you open new credit, or even if someone makes an inquiry about your credit report and score, it causes your score to decrease. And lastly, the credit bureaus are looking for a long payment history so opening a low-limit credit card when you were in college and maintaining it over a long time period and with consistent payments on time will help your score. Interestingly, while it might make good financial sense to close an old credit card account with a retailer you rarely use, you should keep in mind this will likely hurt your credit score. When an account is closed, all of that credit history is removed from your credit report and therefore does not affect your credit score in the future.

6.6   Conclusion: Teachers and Credit

If credit is used responsibly it can allow you to purchase things that might increase in value like a home, paying for them across time. There are many forms of credit and they all have their unique uses. A home mortgage will come with very different terms and interest rates than a personal loan or credit card account. Your ability to get credit depends primarily on your character, capacity to handle credit and any collateral you can supply. Your credit report contains identifying information about you, your credit history, any inquiries made by others for your credit report, and any public records or judgements against you. It does not include your income, race, religion, or assets. Your credit score will be a major determining factor in your ability to receive credit. It is calculated based upon the types of credit you are using, how much new credit you have received, the length of your credit history, the amounts you owe, and your payments history.

6.7   Teacher Tipsheet on Using Credit and Obtaining Debt

- To build a good credit score you need to use credit. Consider a low-limit credit card that you use for only a couple of purchases each month but always pay off the full balance when you are starting your career.

- Check each of your credit reports once per year. You have access to them for free.
- Just because a bank is willing to approve you for a large loan, does not mean you can afford it. You know better than the bank what sorts of monthly payments are affordable for you. Don't borrow more than you need or can afford.
- Always pay your bills on time. If you ever find you missed one by mistake immediately contact the lender and explain the situation before they contact the credit bureaus.
- Shop around for the best loans and credit cards. They are not the same.

6.8 Q&A

1. I make a relatively modest income at my school. Will this keep my credit score low?
   - No! Your credit score does not depend on your income. After you review this chapter you will see that your credit score depends on things like the type of credit you are using, new credit you have applied for or obtained, the length of your credit history, the amounts you owe and your payments history. Put another way, your credit score depends on the choices you make with whatever amount of money you do make.
2. What if I review my credit reports and find a mistake?
   - The law provides individuals with a means of requesting and reviewing their credit report and having a mistake corrected. Although it may take time and patience to correct such errors, it is an important step to take before you apply for a loan. You must contact each credit bureau with a letter in writing that explains the mistake and asks them to make the correction. Sample letters are available online to help you.
3. What is the secret to establishing a good credit score?
   - The secret to establishing good credit is no secret at all. It is really based upon common sense. The key is to live below your means and make the kinds of good financial choices that this book is all about. Some specific ways to establish and keep good credit include:

   i. Pay bills on time.
   ii. Keep balances low on credit cards.
   iii. Apply for new accounts only when necessary.
   iv. Check credit reports for accuracy (once a year is recommended).

v. Never borrow more than you can comfortably pay back.

vi. Borrow only what you need.

vii. Contact lenders immediately if you anticipate a payment problem.

viii. Report lost or stolen credit cards immediately.

6.9   Financial 911 for Teachers

You have a financial 911 when your credit score falls to a level that makes it very difficult for you to obtain credit or any kind. Here are some tips for avoiding this issue:

Pay your bills on time. Missed payments and collections will lower your score substantially. The more payments that are made on time, the better your score. It is likely in your best interest to make the minimum payment on all of your accounts rather than a larger payment to any one creditor.

- Contact your creditors to work out a payment plan. Do not try and avoid them. If you have gotten yourself into trouble, many vendors and credit card companies will be willing to work with you on a payment plan. Don't forget, they want to get paid!
- Stop applying for new credit. Both credit inquiries and new credit lines negatively affect your score.
- Check your credit reports for accuracy. Mistakes do happen and they may be corrected through a letter to the credit bureau you believe to be in error.
- Begin to pay down your credit card balances. High balances on "revolving credit" have a significant and negative impact on your score. You may consider paying off your cards with the highest interest rate first, but another strategy is to take care of the card with the smallest balance and get off to a good start.
- Consider getting some help. There are many qualified agencies that are willing to help you manage your credit situation. The Consumer Credit Counseling Service (credit.org/cccs/) in your area would be a good place to start.

And don't forget that it may feel responsible to close old credit card accounts that you no longer use, but this will lower your credit score as your payment history will be lost forever at a time that you are trying to raise it.

7

Investment Basics for Teachers

7.1 Teacher Case Study: Emma Loves Tech

Emma has been teaching for 5 years. She is the "go to" tech person at George Washington Elementary School. She loves the internet, all of the online learning opportunities for students, and the social media possibilities that go with it all.

Emma and her husband wished to get started saving seriously for their family's future financial goals such as college for the children or retirement but they had not yet gotten around to it.

Emma recently received an inheritance of $20,000 from her grandmother's estate. The arrival of a $20,000 check gave them the motivation get moving to meet their long-term goals. Emma took the lead. She did some online research on stock brokers and found a local one with a good reputation, but then she hesitated. Could she invest her money herself and save on brokerage fees? Emma knew high tech. Her first thought was to buy tech stocks. Facebook, Amazon, Netflix, and Google (the "FANG stocks") were at the top of her list. With an online brokerage account, she could do that herself.

What could go wrong for Emma, in a time when the FANG companies only got more popular every month? A lot could go wrong. Back in the late 1990s when Emma was a little girl, investors were giddy about the potential of the then relatively new internet. Many invested heavily in what were called "dot-com" companies which seemingly could do no wrong. Few expected the merry-go-round to stop, but of course, it did. By one measure, technology stocks lost 72% of their value after a March 2000 peak.

© The Editor(s) (if applicable) and The Author(s), under exclusive license to Springer Nature Switzerland AG 2021
T. Hunt Ferrarini et al., *Teachers Can Be Financially Fit*,
https://doi.org/10.1007/978-3-030-49356-1_7

Emma and her husband went to an investment class at the local community college before making up their minds. The instructor encouraged them not to "put all of their eggs in one basket." The instructor called this diversification. She encouraged them to explore other strategies that would allow them to spread their investments across many sectors. She asked them to consider whether they needed a broker. All of this turned out to be good advice. Read on to learn why.

7.2   Three Rules

There was a smarter finance path for Emma than using a brokerage to put all of the money into FANG companies. She should do better by following three standard rules for building wealth for the long term.

7.2.1   Rule 1: Start Early

Money that's saved early so that it can work for a long time has a great deal of importance in overall wealth building. An early start works so well because of the magic of compounding discussed in Chap. 2. When you save money, you receive a return. In the case of bank accounts, that return is called interest. If you leave the interest in the account, then that money too will earn interest. In other words, you get interest on interest. The longer this process goes on, the more it works for you.

Savings accounts, of course, have relatively low rates of return. However, other investments, such as those in stocks and bonds, can yield higher returns. You get a compound return, or a return on your earlier earned returns. The key is to get started as soon as possible to allow compounding to work for you as long as possible.

This is no get rich quick scheme. Investing for the long term requires patience. Many people are impatient with watching their money build slowly over time. This makes them susceptible to people who promise high returns instantly. But there are no legitimate investments that can promise high returns instantly.

7.2.2 Rule 2: "Buy and Hold"

Buy and hold means that to build wealth over time, you have to hold on to your long-term investments. You can't be dipping into them, or they won't compound over time in the same way.

To buy and hold, you have to have your finances in order. Here's what you have to do:

- In order to accomplish anything financially, you have to spend less than you receive. Stay with your spending plan (see Chap. 2) so that you can "pay yourself first" with savings that can be allocated to your long-term investments.
- Avoid excessive debt. Manage your credit properly. For example, limit the number of credit cards you have. Limit your purchases to what you can pay off each month, without leaving a balance to accumulate interest that you'll also have to pay. If you have a lot of student loan debt, skip to Chap. 10 to see how Margaret addressed the problem. As time goes by, your credit score goes up, making it possible for you to borrow at lower rates if you have a good reason to borrow.
- Set up an emergency fund (also addressed in Chap. 2). This is income you set aside for unexpected expenses such as medical bills or a loss of income. If you don't have a fund for unexpected expenses, it will be hard to buy and hold. You might, for example, have to dip into the children's college fund to pay for a big car repair. Not good. This slows down the compounding process. You may have to build up the emergency fund gradually, but the rule of thumb is to have 3–6 months income set aside.

Buy and hold means that you are contributing to your long-term investments for the over time, regardless of what is going on in, say, the stock markets or bond markets. It is sometimes called "dollar-cost averaging." Dollar-cost averaging means investing a fixed amount of money in the same fund at regular intervals over a long period of time.

"Buy and hold" and dollar cost averaging are especially good advice for teachers like Emma. She has a busy life and cannot spend much time monitoring how her investments are doing. As it turns out, Emma will do better if she mostly just lets them grow. Here's why: When financial markets are down, she is buying for less. When financial markets are up, those inexpensively bought investments are worth more. And, the process just keeps going.

When she first received her inheritance check, Emma wondered if she could be a "day trader" in tech stocks. Day traders try to jump in the market with their savings when prices are low and out of the market when prices are high, even though regulations made it somewhat difficult to play the market with that money. Emma at first thought she might be able to "buy low" and "sell high" because of her knowledge of technology. But then she thought about how wrapped up she is the entire time she is at school. She cannot be constantly checking her stocks while teaching her classes. Emma was relieved when she learned that day trading doesn't work as well as staying with the dull rule, "buy and hold." She was ready to be dull with her financial future.

7.2.3 Rule 3: Diversify

After she learned more, Emma realized it would have been a mistake to invest all of her $20,000 into one industry. Although her investment class was very short, it taught her to diversify. That means to take on many small risks rather than one large risk.

Consider how much you risk when you fail to diversify. If you put all of your savings into a new start-up artificial intelligence company, you could get rich if the company succeeds. Or you could lose everything if the company fails. The same point would apply if you were approached by someone proposing that you invest in a business opportunity. If you put all your saved money there, you would again be putting your money at risk. That's dangerous. It's far safer to spread risks out. This means holding a variety of financial assets rather than just one. (Jump ahead in this Chapter to learn about index funds and other ways to diversify your investments.)

You might be good at figuring this out yourself but many people depend on the assistance of a financial advisor to help them diversify. See the Teacher Tipsheet for more on financial advisors.

What is your tolerance for risk? The key to investing wisely is understanding that there is a trade-off between risk and return. The greater the risk, the greater the potential return. Risk is the chance that an investment will earn less than anticipated or will even lose money.

When deciding how much risk to take on, you should consider your tolerance for risk and your time horizon. Risk tolerance is your ability and willingness to lose some or all of your investment in exchange for potentially greater returns. If you won't be able to sleep at night worrying about the downside of your investments, then you have a low risk tolerance. If this is you, maybe you want to look for lower returns that allow you to rest easy at night. In contrast, if you don't panic even when your investments are headed in the wrong direction, then you have a higher risk tolerance and are more willing to weather storms in hopes of larger returns in the future.

The amount of risk you are willing to take also depends on your time horizon, which is the number of months or years you plan to keep the investment. Longer-term investments can be volatile. Vanguard and many others report that the average annual rate of return on stocks is about 7% after correcting for inflation. But, the long-term average annual return masks the ups and downs you will face. Stocks can lose big—40% or more—in some years. But if you have a long-time horizon, you can ride out this volatility.

Right now, Emma is a relatively young teacher. She and her husband can afford to take higher risks. As retirement age approaches, they might shift over to investments offering less risk because they would then have less time to recover from an adverse stock or bond market.

There are many types of investment risk. Here are three.

- *Market price risk* is the chance that the price of an investment will decrease in price. Stock prices, for example, move up and down even when the long-term trend is up.
- *Inflation risk* is the possibility that the return on an investment will be less than inflation as measured by the Consumer Price Index. You want your investments to, at least, beat inflation or you are losing ground.
- *Interest rate risk* is the risk that declining interest rates will hurt your investments, particularly in bonds.

Financial advisors typically ask clients to complete a survey on risk tolerance which, in turn, will influence what sort of investments the advisor will suggest. The survey is repeated several times with changing age and other circumstances. You can find commonly used surveys online. They often pose statements and responses like these:

- I prefer investments with little fluctuation in value, and I am willing to accept lower returns associated with these sorts of investments (strongly agree, agree, disagree, strongly disagree).
- If I owned a stock investment that lost 30% of its value in 3 months I would (sell all of it, sell some of it, hold it and stand pat, buy more of it.)
- During market declines, I prefer to sell some of my riskier investments and move them into safer investments (strongly agree, agree, disagree, strongly disagree).

7.3   Forms of Saving and Investing – Safe Investments

Some teachers make the mistake of keeping all of their money in the safest forms of assets. Although they don't face much risk of loss, they greatly reduce what their money can earn over the long run. To make the best decisions, you need to know about the assets you can choose when you're thinking about where to put your money. We'll start with the safest kinds, and then proceed to some riskier ones.

7.3.1   Savings Accounts

These accounts are kept at banks and credit unions. They are most appropriate for savings you may need in the short term. They allow you to access your money quickly and without penalty. This is a highly liquid form of savings, meaning can get to your cash quickly. Savings accounts are insured by the Federal Deposit Insurance Corporation (FDIC), and no one has ever lost even a penny of federally-insured individual savings deposits. Your money will be safe in a savings account. But, *because* the money in a savings account is so safe and can be withdrawn without penalty at any time, there is not much return. The interest paid on savings is small but steady. Savings accounts are a great place to keep your emergency fund.

7.3.2   Certificates of Deposit

Just like savings accounts, certificates of deposit (often called CDs) are offered by banks and credit unions and are federally insured. When you buy a certificate of deposit, you are tying your money up for a specified period — from one month to a number of years. Unlike a savings account, your savings in a CD are less liquid, that means it's harder to spend than money from a checking or savings account. Before spending it, you have to wait until the term is up — or be assessed interest penalties for an early withdrawal. In return for giving the bank longer use of your money, you get somewhat higher interest than the rates paid on a savings account. You can search online to find the most favorable interest rates for CDs.

7.3.3 Money Market Mutual Funds

Mutual funds pool together the funds of many investors and use the money to purchase assets. A *money market* mutual fund uses the funds to purchase U.S. Treasury bills and commercial paper (short-term debt from corporations.) Even though money market mutual funds are sold by banks (and other financial institutions) they are not insured by the FDIC. These accounts offer easy access to your money. Many include checking accounts. There is some risk but historically, it has been low. Money market mutual funds might be another place to build cash for your emergency fund or money for other short-term saving goals.

7.4 Forms of Saving and Investing – Riskier Investments

Now, let's move to longer term saving and investment alternatives that are designed to grow your money over time.

7.4.1 Bonds

When you buy a bond, you are, in effect, making a loan to the issuer of the bond. You are lending your money to the government, a government agency, or a corporation that issued the bond. The bond will specify under what terms your money is repaid and what the interest will be. Bonds pay a fixed interest rate and they have a maturity date when the principal (the money you used to buy the bond) will be repaid. Some bonds are very safe, such as those issued by the federal government. Government bonds are regarded as being nearly liquid because there is usually a willing buyer if you decide to sell.

Some bonds have medium safety, such as those issued by major corporations. Almost certainly, you'll get your money back with interest, but there's a chance that a major corporation could fail. Finally, some bonds are known as "junk bonds." Junk bonds are high risk investments. There is a real probability that the companies issuing them may not be able pay investors back.

Bonds are traded in bond markets. They can be bought or sold before the maturity date. Bond prices depend on interest rates and the financial strength of the issuer. Prices of existing bonds rise when interest rates decline. Prices of existing bonds fall when interest rates rise.

7.4.2   Stocks

When you buy a stock, you become a shareholder and a part-owner of a corporation. That is easy to see when four people contribute equally to a new corporation and each owns a fourth of the venture. All four would share in the profits of the business and all four would have a fourth of the decision-making authority.

Modern corporations issue millions of shares, but the principle is the same. If a corporation has 200 million shares of stock out, then buying a share makes you a 1200-millionth owner of the corporation. You have a claim on 1200-millionth of the worth of the corporation, and you have 1200-millionth of the decision-making authority in the corporation. Like bonds, there are usually willing buyers of stocks so they are considered to be liquid assets.

Shareholders can benefit in two ways from owning shares of stock. First, shareholders benefit if the price of their shares increase. If you buy and hold stocks for the long term, you are anticipating that the value of your shares will increase over time. If you sell, that is called a capital gain. However, if the price of your shares decreases and you sell, that is called a capital loss. Second, some corporations distribute profits to shareholders in the form of dividends. Dividend payments are an important source of income. This is especially the case for many people who are in retirement.

But, of all the assets discussed, stocks carry the highest risk. A company could have great success, increasing the value to the investment to shareholders. Or it could fail, making its shareholders suffer losses.

7.4.3   Real Estate

When you purchase a home, it is historically regarded as a safe investment. You pay your mortgage and you get a place to live. Over time, its value will likely go up and you will pay down the amount of the loan plus interest.

It is also possible to invest in real estate as a landlord. You might buy half of a duplex and rent it out, for example. Being a landlord can be rewarding, but there are risks to investing in real estate (other than your own home). You are responsible for the upkeep on the rental property, and finding renters who will pay rent on time can be a hassle. If something breaks, you have to fix it or hire someone to fix it. If a renter is late with a monthly payment, that doesn't excuse you from making mortgage payments to the bank. Finally, real estate is regarded as a non-liquid asset because it can take months to sell the property.

7.5 Risk and Reward

We have already explained why safe investments do not offer big returns. If you choose the safety of a bank account for your money, you won't earn a lot of interest but you will have easy access to your money. Alternatively, riskier investments offer the possibility of larger returns. If they did not, nobody would invest in them. As we move from bank assets to bonds to stocks and real estate, we're moving toward assets with many possibilities for things to go wrong — and for things to go right. A company whose stock you buy may succeed wildly or go bankrupt, or anything in between. You take that risk when you own a single company's stock.

Look at the pyramid in Fig. 7.1. At the bottom of the pyramid there are safe ways to keep money. They have lower returns than the riskier investments toward the top. In investing, you should build the bottom of the pyramid with safe investments like bank accounts and CDs first. Later you can venture into riskier stocks and bonds closer to the top of the pyramid.

Fig. 7.1 Risk and reward

7.6   Mutual Funds

How do we get a high return while managing the risk? The answer lies in adhering to Rule 3 on diversification. When you diversify, you take a lot of small risks rather than a single large risk. The small risks do not add up to much, and they get smaller and smaller over time for an investor who buys and holds on to a variety of financial assets.

You might think of diversifying by buying small amounts of a lot of different stocks and bonds. But because it costs something to buy each asset, that approach would quickly get to be expensive. Emma's $20,000 might seem like a lot, but it does not go very far if she is trying to diversify by picking individual stocks and bonds. Fortunately, there are mutual funds that act to buy financial assets on behalf of individual investors.

A mutual fund obtains a pool of money by accepting funds from thousands of individual investors. It invests its pool of money into a collection of assets. As that collection generates income, the mutual fund sends that income back to its investors in proportion to how much money they have put in. Because of its large size, a mutual fund can efficiently buy large numbers of different stocks and bonds.

People who invest in diversified mutual funds have their savings spread out over several sectors such as energy, financials, industrials, utilities, information technology, telecommunications, consumer discretionary, consumer staples, health care, and more. And, they can spread over different types of companies and government assets including companies regarded as small stock, large stock, and international as well as long-term government bonds and treasury bills. If Emma's $20,000 goes into a diversified mutual fund, she and her spouse are spreading out their investment over many alternatives. In any one year, some will do well and others may do poorly but being diversified reduces the risk of losses.

Emma must remember that mutual funds are nowhere near as safe as bank deposits. When asset markets go down, mutual funds follow them down, depending on which stocks and bonds they're holding. Over time, however, mutual funds have been an excellent investment, far surpassing bank accounts and bonds in their long-term returns. Many people without special financial knowledge—teachers, firefighters and mechanics—have become financially secure by starting early, buying and holding, and using mutual funds to diversify.

After learning about the benefits of mutual funds, Emma came back around to the question of a financial adviser. Did she need one? A financial adviser would help her pick mutual funds, but with no guarantee that the mutual funds would do better than funds she might choose herself. Those funds might have loads (or sales commissions). Such funds are called load funds. Many of them are actively managed, meaning that they try to earn a rate of return that is greater than the market average.

What to do? On reading further, Emma found out about a kind of mutual fund that does not try to beat the market return and instead settles for matching the return, as represented by a collection of stocks. These so-called "index funds" try to replicate a market average such as the Standard and Poor's 500 stock index or the total stock average. Because the composition of the index is clear, it costs less to manage an index fund than an actively managed fund. Lower expenses would mean more of the investment was working for Emma's future.

Emma made the decision to put the $20,000 into low-cost index funds from a well-respected financial firm. Emma was smart to make these decisions by taking the class and doing her research—but if she felt insecure, going with a financial adviser would have been a good move. A good financial adviser would have strongly discouraged her from day trading and would have put her into diversified mutual funds rather than getting her into picking stocks. Either way, Emma had avoided two opposite mistakes: taking too much risk by being a day trader, and taking too little risk by leaving the money in the bank. (Learn more about selecting financial advisers in Chap. 1.)

7.7 Exchange Traded Funds (ETFs)

For beginning or small investors, mutual funds are just the ticket. Those who become familiar with mutual funds, however, may wish to investigate exchange traded funds. An ETF is a close relative to a mutual fund that offers more flexibility. The ETF, like a mutual fund, owns a collection of underlying assets such as stock, bonds, oil futures, gold bars, or foreign currency. It divides ownership of those assets into shares. Like many mutual funds, the ETF may track an index or a category of assets. Unlike a mutual fund, the ETF trades like a stock. ETFs tend to be more liquid and have lower fees than mutual funds. ETFs also can provide diversification.

7.8   Conclusion: Teachers and Financial Security

You didn't enter into teaching to get rich. Maybe you are a little offended by friends or family members who seem to pursue money as if other things didn't matter. Got it! Nonetheless, we suggest that being financially secure allows you to relax and feel good about your future. It also allows you to be generous to support your children with their educations, meet other family obligations, and make contributions to your community or church. These good things are nearly impossible if you are not financially secure. People who live paycheck-to-paycheck rarely can be financially charitable to others. The good news is that even a teacher with a busy professional schedule can increase the chances of being financially secure. Remember our three rules? Start early. Buy and hold. Diversify. Following these rules takes some self-discipline but it does not require closely tracking financial markets. As your money grows, you can then get down to the serious business of allocating your money to achieve your short-term and long-term financial goals.

7.9   Teacher Tipsheet on Building Wealth for the Long Term

1. Get rich quick schemes rarely work. You need to have patience and persistence to achieve financial security.
2. Know your tolerance for risk. If you are single, maybe that is easy. If you are married, it might be harder because each spouse may have a different risk tolerance. Hopefully, some honest discussion and research can result in agreement.
3. Remember that you need savings for short-term and long-term purposes. Start at the bottom of the pyramid in Fig. 7.1 and move up as soon as you feel confident enough to proceed.
4. Give serious consideration to investing in indexed stock mutual funds. These are relatively low cost and they beat the return of almost all actively managed stock mutual funds.
5. Buy and hold but remember to change things up periodically. Your investments probably need to shift as your children grow up and you get older.
6. If you are intimidated at going it alone, consider choosing a financial advisor. Do your research to select someone who understands your circumstances. Be sure to ask how much he or she charges. Planning fee? Commission? Percentage of assets?

7.10   Q&A

1. I didn't start early. Is there any hope for me?
   – Yes, but it is a little harder. The point is to get the miracle of compound interest working for you as soon as possible. If you turn over to Chap. 8 and Chap. 9, you will see how retirement accounts are structured. Retirement plans like 403(b)s and Individual Retirement Accounts (IRAS) allow people who are starting to save later in their careers to contribute more than others. You probably will not get completely caught up, but you will be better off financially than if you fail to act.
2. What if I have a financial emergency? Isn't dipping into my long-term savings better than, say, taking on a lot of credit card debt to get me over the hump?
   – Neither alternative is a good financial move. The best thing is to do get into the habit of putting some portion of each paycheck into a savings account or a money market mutual fund for use as an emergency fund. Take it step by step. And, remember, you won't experience an emergency during every pay period. The longer you go paying money in and not having to take money out, the sooner you can have 3 or 4 months of income in the bank and standing ready if you need it. That can buy you a lot of peace of mind.
3. If wealth building is as easy as following three rules, why are so many people just living paycheck to paycheck?
   – Saving is like exercise. We all know that regular exercise provides many benefits like weight loss, a healthier heart, less stress, and more energy. However, these benefits come primarily after you have been doing regular exercise for at least a few weeks. If fact, the first days in the gym can be frustrating, painful, and expensive. When to the costs of exercise occur? Now! But, when do the benefits occur? In the future! That gives people an incentive to not get started. Saving works the same way. The benefits appear in the future as you notice your long-term investment accounts starting to take off. But the costs occur now. Those items you decide not to buy today (taking the family to a popular movie, a great meal at a trendy restaurant, a long weekend get-a-way) are immediate sacrifices that you make today in hopes of gaining a more secure financial future. When the costs are real and immediate and the benefits are uncertain and, in the future, people sometimes make poor financial choices. We think that is why some people choose to ignore our simple three rules for building wealth. We hope that reading the chapters in this book helps you see how the benefits of following our simple rules far outweigh the costs.

7.11   Financial 911 for Teachers

You have a financial 911 when the stock market declines and you see your financial security slipping away. The longest running bull market came to an abrupt end in mid-March of 2020 with the outbreak of the coronavirus pandemic. The Dow Jones Industrial Average (DJIA) dropped 3000 points in one day! The economic damage caused by the coronavirus pandemic was enormous.

But we have seen a version of this movie before. The stock market crash of 2008 occurred on September 29, 2008. The DJIA fell nearly 800 points and kept going down until March of 2009, when it bottomed out. It took years to make up for the damage, but since then the market has not only recovered but reached new highs.

But, what did many teachers do as they watched the markets plunge? They sold their stocks but at very low prices. That panic reaction is certainly understandable. For teachers close to retirement, they felt the need to stop the bleeding to preserve what they had left. But, what about other younger teachers who had a longer time horizon? Many of them not only stayed in the market, they continued to buy more. After all, it looked to them like stocks were on sale. Time to buy low and wait for the markets to recover.

Teachers who stayed (remember the rule buy and hold?) did well. They recovered from all of their losses and then when share prices began to rise, they were far ahead of the game. In any future market crash, there's no guarantee that share prices will recover quickly. The one guarantee is that those who sell in the initial panic lock in their losses. That's why we, the authors of this book, don't just recommend buy and hold – we practice it.

8

Retirement for Public School Teachers

8.1 Teacher Case Study: Tom Turns Out to Be Terrific at Getting a Comfortable Retirement

Tom has been teaching ninth grade civics for 10 years. He did not go into teaching to become rich. However, he and his family (working spouse and three children) have lived comfortably over the past few years since Tom earned his national teacher certification and master's degree. He was, it seems, just cut out to be a great classroom teacher. It is what he loves. He is not going to go into school administration, nor is he likely to leave the profession. Now, he has realized that if he is going to retire as a classroom teacher, he needs to make sure he is on the right track.

Tom knows that he has a state pension which is call a "defined benefit plan." It is called that because the state has specified, or defined, the exact formula that will determine how much money Tom receives in retirement. The state is then responsible for coming up with that money. Tom can get a solid estimate of the amount his monthly retirement check will be for the rest of his life with just few clicks at the state teacher retirement website. In this way, Tom is a lucky guy. Most of Tom's friends and family members have what are called "defined contribution" plans. That means they know how much they are contributing to their retirement savings with their employer, but they don't know how much they will have in retirement payouts. The exact amount depends on how well their investments perform over the long term.

T. Hunt Ferrarini et al., *Teachers Can Be Financially Fit*, https://doi.org/10.1007/978-3-030-49356-1_8

Tom is on track for a comfortable retirement, even though he never set out to be terrific at retirement planning. He lives in a state with a solvent retirement system. He will probably opt for a modest but dependable monthly annuity payment. He also pays into Social Security (not available to teachers in all states). That will be another source of cash flow in retirement. Tom's home mortgage will be paid off before he hits retirement age. He has some additional savings in his 403 (b) account with the school district as well as a Roth Individual Retirement Account (IRA). (See Chap. 9 to learn more about these options.) Finally, Tom's state provides for generous health insurance coverage for retired teachers and their dependents. In fact, Tom will probably have a net worth (assets minus liabilities) of a million dollars when he retires. Not bad. Tom is in better shape for retirement than many of his non-teacher friends.

8.2   How a Traditional Teacher Pension Works

The Bureau of Labor Statistics reports that 89% of public-school teachers participate in a defined benefit pension plan. That figure is down slightly from earlier years. This is due to some states trying to move teachers into other retirement options in order to cut costs. Most of these resemble some sort of a 401(k) plan similar to what private sector employees have. (See Chap. 9 to learn more about tax advantaged retirement accounts.)

Most public-school teachers will have three sources of income in retirement: payments from the state retirement system, Social Security (if eligible), and personal savings. For most teachers, the state pension is an important part of the retirement picture. It can provide a lifetime income during retirement, and depending which payout option is selected, it may even continue to others after death. The size of the monthly benefit is determined by many factors, including years of teaching, salary while working, age at retirement, and so forth.

8.3   Retirement Realities: Understanding Teacher Plans

Reading this chapter is a great start. You will then need to get information and then understand that there are different types of retirement plans. You want to make informed choices.

1. The first step is to get information. You should then visit the website of your state teacher retirement system to find out more about how your state system operates. With this background, you should then schedule a visit with a retirement counselor. This person may be in Human Resources at your school system—or your HR office may refer you directly to the state retirement office. In any event, you should find out who your retirement counselor is. Then you can set up a visit to find out how the benefits of the retirement plan apply to your individual situation. Don't be shy about asking. They are people whose job it is to counsel people like you.

2. State retirement programs are not all the same. Pension programs vary from state to state. While many state pension programs share similar features, the details widely vary. Some states (California, Illinois, New York, and Ohio) offer teachers generous benefits while others (Wisconsin and Florida) offer more modest plans. Some states have very well managed and well-funded systems and others are less well managed and seriously underfunded. Some states' plans may even not be sustainable over the long term.

3. State teacher pensions are funded by individual and employer contributions – and so are inevitably subject to politics. Teachers' pensions are funded by some combination of individual contributions and employer contributions. The amount of the contribution rates varies and may change.

   State teacher pensions are subject to politics in a way that individually held retirement accounts are not. Teachers' contributions are pooled into a fund that is managed by a state board. Since everyone does not draw retirement payments out at once, the contributions are invested in stocks and bonds. A well-managed pension fund should be taking in more contributions and investment earnings than it pays out. The amount of money in the pension fund will have ups and downs with changes in the stock and bond markets but the payouts should be sustainable over the long term. Depending on how the political winds blow, pension terms may become more or less generous. Because teacher pensions are a substantial component of state spending, they are a likely political target—but politicians also understand that teachers vote in large numbers and will not easily accept reductions in promised benefits.

4. If you leave teaching to pursue other opportunities, you have some choices to make. If you leave teaching before minimum retirement age in your state and you are vested in the retirement system, you can either leave your money in the system to grow or close your account. To be vested means that you gain ownership of your retirement account. States establish a minimum number of years of residential teaching in order for you to be vested.

It usually takes as few as 3 years or as long to 10 years to be vested. This is important information for you to learn.

If you leave your money in the system, when you reach retirement age you will be potentially eligible for a pension check for the rest of your life. It might be a relatively small amount, but it could be a nice bump to your retirement income. If you close the account, you can request a lump-sum payout.

5. A formula is used to determine your basic retirement benefits, but you still have some choices to make. Each state has established a formula which is used to calculate your benefits. It usually depends on the following:

   – Years of service
   – Final average monthly earnings
   – Other factors such as years of consecutive service, total earnings, or the highest earnings you achieved for a set number of years.

   Most state teacher retirement websites have a calculator that allows you to estimate the amount of your pension payout.

   But wait. That is only the beginning of the story. Your initial estimate of your pension benefit provides you with a single life option or the maximum amount you can receive from the state retirement system. For many teachers this may not be the best option. Tom, for example, is married. He would like his spouse to continue to receive a pension check if he dies before she does. In this case, it is common to select a joint and survivor option. This means that, regardless of who dies first, the surviving spouse continues to receive a pension payout. However, to gain this advantage, the monthly payment itself would be less than under the single life alternative.

6. You may be able to choose a partial or total lump-sum withdrawal. Most plans allow for lump-sum withdrawals. You can choose to have part or all of your retirement account balance paid directly to you. If your state's fund is not well-funded, it may make sense to take the lump sum rather than a monthly payout. No one wants to face a situation, 5 years into retirement, of getting a letter stating that your pension is cut in half (or worse than that, if your state's plan fails financially).

   But if your state retirement fund is healthy, you should think twice about taking a lump-sum payment. It may look like a lot and it may be tempting to tap your retirement savings for today's expenses but that was not the goal of paying into your pension. Your pension is intended to provide you with income for a secure retirement. That could, and hopefully will, stretch into many years. Plus, taxes and early payout penalties could greatly reduce the amount of cash. Once you have made your payout selection, your choice is almost certainly irrevocable. Unfortunately, once you make your payout selection, you can't go back 3 years later and say, "I took the single life annuity only but now I want to change that to protect my spouse." Check your state plan's website and you'll likely find out that this decision is irrevocable.

you will receive.

7. Pension payouts are subject to ordinary income taxes. The money in your retirement account is pretax money, meaning it has never been taxed. When you take a payout, you will be responsible for paying the taxes you owe on that money. Just as is true now when you're working, your age and personal financial situation will determine the amount of tax due. (Some states have tax breaks for retirees that will apply to you, just as to every other retiree, and the federal tax code has some modest tax breaks for those over 65.)

8. Double dipping may be a good way to supplement your income in retirement. Some teachers decide to return to work for schools while still collecting their pensions, a practice sometimes referred to as "double dipping." It is not uncommon for teachers to return to the classroom as substitute teachers, for example. It is no surprise that teacher might want to earn a little extra income in retirement and keep that involvement in the lives of young people and teacher colleagues. But the decision to return to work needs to be taken with some caution. Most states have rules about this which might involve, for example, blackout periods before returning to work. Violating the rules might put your retirement benefits in jeopardy. You should check this out with your retirement counselor before making the decision to return to work for a school or other agency that falls under the state retirement system. Breaking the rules many cost you your benefits.

8.4   When Should You Retire?

That is a question only you can answer but there are many things to consider. Many states and school districts permit teachers to retirement as early as age 55 and still receive benefits.

In most cases, it probably makes sense to remain teaching until you hit the retirement age established by your state or school. Most often, if you retire before that age, you will not receive full benefits. But there are many factors to consider as you ponder when to leave the profession. First, do you still enjoy teaching (and do the students still seem to enjoy you?). If you still love the students, contact with colleagues, and your subject, why rush? However, if you are tired of some of the things that come with teaching (record keeping, grading papers, discipline issues, dealing with parents, and so forth), maybe you want to leave early, even if you won't have full benefits. Second, are you healthy? If you are concerned that you might not be able to enjoy many years in retirement, maybe you want to pull early. Third, some states offer financial incentives to retire early. The idea is to encourage teachers with higher salaries to leave early to save money. If you are going to make close to the same amount of income without showing up for first period class every day, it would be hard to resist taking an early retirement. Finally, let's circle back to the first thing we mentioned: get information. Retirement benefits can vary from state to state, district to district, and even school to school. You need to do the research to find out what is best for you.

8.5   Understand Your Social Security Choices

Most teachers pay into Social Security. In addition to a state retirement plan, this can provide another guaranteed cash flow for you in retirement. However, according to Bellwether Education Partners, about 40% of public-school teachers, or about 1.2 million teachers nationwide, are not covered by Social Security. Those teachers are concentrated in 15 states — Alaska, California, Colorado, Connecticut, Georgia, Illinois, Kentucky, Louisiana, Maine, Massachusetts, Missouri, Nevada, Ohio, Rhode Island, and Texas—and the District of Columbia, where many or all public-school teachers neither pay into nor receive benefits from Social Security. Teachers in those states face more financial uncertainty. They may need to rely more heavily on their state pensions or personal savings. Some will need to consider working after retirement.

One of the authors recently overheard this comment in a South Florida diner: "I am sure having trouble making ends meet living on Social Security." Well, yes you are. Social Security was never intended to be the sole source of retirement income. It was intended to provide a very basic income so that people would not be destitute in retirement. Living on Social Security as a sole source of income would be very difficult and, thankfully, most teachers are not in that situation.

What do you contribute to Social Security? Currently, you and your employer each pay a 6.2% Social Security tax on up to $132,900 of your earnings and a 1.45% Medicare tax on all your earnings. If you are one of those teachers who run a business, on that income you pay the combined employee and employer amount. That's a 12.4% Social Security tax on up to $132,900 of your net earnings and a 2.9% Medicare tax on your entire net earnings.

To begin getting a handle on your Social Security benefits, let's find out how much you have paid in to Social Security over the years. Visit the Social Security Administration (SSA) to learn about your earnings history. Go to ssa.gov/myaccount. Open an account. Then, click on your Earnings Record. Here you will find your taxed Social Security earnings and your taxed Medicare earnings listed by each work year. You will also find the total estimated Social Security taxes paid by you and your employers as well as the total estimated Medicare taxes paid by you and your employers. It is probably a good idea to review your Earning Record periodically to make sure there are no mistakes.

The SSA has several calculators at ssa.gov to help you plan for retirement. Here are two examples of calculators you might wish to use. First, the SSA provides a Retirement Estimator. It uses your Earnings Record to estimate your monthly Social Security benefit. Your benefits calculation is based on your highest 35 years of income. Second, there is a Life Expectancy Calculator which also provides information about when to begin taking your Social Security benefits. This is important because your monthly benefits will be reduced if you retire before your full retirement age.

Deciding at what age to begin drawing Social Security is a serious decision. You can begin receiving Social Security as early as age 62. But, the amount of your benefit will be less than if you wait to your full retirement age. If you can delay even longer, say to age 70, your Social Security benefit for the rest of your life will be larger still.

Finally, you should pay close attention to the rules for collecting Social Security while still working. If you are collecting Social Security at certain ages, there is a limit on how much income you can earn. As an example, for a 64-year-old earning more than $17,040 in 2018, the Social Security System will deduct one dollar for every three dollars earned about the limit. After you reach your Social Security "full retirement" age, however, there is no income limit. The full retirement age for those retiring in 2018 is 66. This age gradually rises to 67 by the year 2027.

8.6   Considering Other Sources of Income

Another retirement savings alternative is to consider establishing a 403(b) plan with your school district. In a 403(b), money for retirement is taken out of your paycheck, not taxed, and invested for retirement. State and school district policies regarding 403(b) plans vary widely. In most cases, the policy is decided by the local school district. Some states and school districts allow all qualified financial companies to offer 403(b) accounts. Other states and school districts limit the number of companies. The best advice here is the make an appointment with a human resource specialist in your school district to learn what your alternatives might be. There is more discussion of 403(b) plans in Chap. 9.

8.7   Conclusion: Teachers and Financial Security

Many teachers do not consider themselves to be well compensated for their work. We get that. However, public school teachers across the nation have access to state teacher retirement programs which still offer lifetime payouts. This makes retirement planning a lot simpler. The state puts money away on your behalf and invests it for you. But your retirement planning is not exactly on auto-pilot. There are decisions that still need to be made regarding how you will arrange your retirement payout. Most of these decisions are irrevocable.

Most teacher retirement plans are not intended to be the sole source of income. Social Security can help. And, it is important to accumulate other personal savings perhaps by setting up a 403(b) plan with your school district and establishing a Roth IRA. Learn more about additional saving for retirement options in the next chapter.

8.8   Teacher Tipsheet on Public School Teacher Retirement

- Having a state teacher retirement pension plan has helped millions of teachers to have a comfortable retirement.
- Know how your state retirement system works. You can learn a lot from the state retirement website but eventually you should speak to a retirement counselor who works for the system.

- Be especially careful when you decide how to receive your retirement payout. The decision is irrevocable.
- Double dipping might be a great alternative to earn a little extra money and still enjoy retirement. But, know the rules so you don't threaten your state or Social Security benefits.
- Be sure to consider using other forms of personal savings such as a 403 (b) plan or a Roth IRA.
- Smile. You have more security in your retirement because you have a defined benefit pension plan. The vast majority of people working in the private sector do not have this option.

8.9   Q&A

1. Are all teachers eligible for state pensions?
   - Not exactly. The majority of states require teachers to serve for 5 years before qualifying for a pension, and 16 states require teachers to serve for 10 years. Teachers do not always remain in the profession. Those that leave before they are vested will not receive a lifetime pension at retirement. Traditional teacher retirement systems tend to reward stability and length of service.
2. Are state retirement plans portable to other states?
   - No. Teachers can remain in the teacher retirement system if they move from one public school district to another within the state. However, they can't continue to pay into the system if the leave the state or leave teaching entirely.
3. Why are several states moving toward a 401(k) defined contribution style programs?
   - Most states have not adequately funded their teacher retirement programs. Absent significant policy reforms, unfunded liabilities of state teacher retirement programs will continue to grow and threaten the long-term financial security of teacher pensions as well as taxpayers. In most cases states offer new teachers what is called a hybrid plan, which combines elements of a traditional pension and a 401(k)-style account. The amount of the state contribution is reduced and individual teachers, rather than a state board, make the investment decisions. Some teachers might appreciate having greater control over their retirement savings. Others fear that the change to a defined contribution plan will add to uncertainly and result in lower benefits.

4. Will Social Security be there for me?
   - Yes, and here's why: Although Social Security is underfunded—not able to fully pay all promised benefits without reform—it does have sufficient resources to pay a stable 75% of promised benefits out to 2035 and beyond. So even in the scenario in which nothing is done, you would get the majority of promised benefits. However, Social Security is one of the most popular federal programs and it commands wide support. Therefore, a solution is likely. Finally, even in the unlikely case that funding is not beefed up, the partial benefits paid would most likely be complete for those of low and middle incomes, and then tapered off for higher-income recipients (a policy known as "means testing.")

8.10   Financial 911 for Teachers

You may have a financial 911 if you teach in a state with a severely underfunded teacher retirement program. The worst-case scenario is that your state's plan fails when you are retired, or so close to retirement that you have little opportunity to react. How likely is a state plan's failure? According to the National Council on Teacher Quality, in most states, the current teacher pension system is unsustainable and can't be fixed without comprehensive policy changes. Nationwide just 11 states—Alaska, Illinois, Maine, Minnesota, New Hampshire, New Jersey, Rhode Island, South Dakota, Utah, Washington, and Wisconsin—meet any of the four goals (flexibility, sustainability, neutrality, or transparency) for teacher pension health, and no state meets them all. In 2016, just seven states had teacher retirement plans that were funded at 90% or higher. South Dakota and Wisconsin are the only two states in the nation with fully-funded teacher retirement programs. At 42%, Illinois continues to have the lowest funded pension system in the nation.

What might you do if you teach in an underfunded state? Your options are few and limited:

- Move to a state with a sound teacher pension plan, paying due attention to getting certified to teach in that state. (For many teachers this is unrealistic, but for those teaching in a major metro area close to state lines, it's a real possibility.)
- Take more control over your own retirement by increasing your contributions to optional plans in which you own your account (such as 403(b) plans. Such plans are unaffected by teacher pension problems.

- Make sure that, as a family, you're taking maximum advantage of available retirement plans. Your spouse may have a favorable 401(k) plan at another workplace that can add to family retirement security. Even if your spouse is not working outside the home, Individual Retirement Account (IRAs) contributions can be made on a tax-advantaged basis. (Learn more about IRAs in Chap. 9.)
- When possible, take your retirement benefits as a lump sum rather than arranging for extended benefits from a shaky state system. (Make sure to "roll over" the lump sum into a qualified plan like an IRA. Don't ever take possession of that money, or you may owe a big tax bill).
- Become an advocate for pension reform in your state. There are limits on what any one teacher can do in a highly political environment, but voters need to understand that real people will be hurt if teacher pension "reform" becomes, in actuality, pension reduction or even default.
- Recognize that even in the worst case your benefits are unlikely to disappear altogether. Political solutions to big defaults tend to involve sharing the pain rather than concentrating it on any one group.

9

Saving for Retirement: Options for Charter and Private School Teachers

9.1   Teacher Case Study: Donna

Donna teaches math in an inner-city charter school. Most of her students come from single-family households and most are poor: Over 90% of them are eligible for free or reduced lunch.

Great math teachers at schools like Donna's are rare. But Donna is a gifted teacher. She loves math and she loves her students. She believes that building strong math skills is the gateway out of poverty, and she has high expectations of her students.

But as dedicated as Donna is to her students and to teaching them to work towards a more financially secure future, she is not doing the same for herself. In fact, she is not saving a thing for her own retirement. She's been teaching for 15 years and barely has anything to show for it financially. Also working against Donna is that charter school teachers in her state are not allowed to participate in the state teacher retirement program. As a way to compensate for this, the Board of the charter school offers its teachers the chance to participate in a 403(b) retirement plan. The Board matches up to 5% of what teachers contribute to their 403(b). But Donna has never enrolled in the program. Not only is she passing up a tax-advantaged way to save for retirement, but she is literally leaving the school Board's matching contribution money on the table.

T. Hunt Ferrarini et al., *Teachers Can Be Financially Fit*,
https://doi.org/10.1007/978-3-030-49356-1_9

9.2   Charter School Teachers

Charter schools are publicly funded but independently managed, so they occupy a middle ground between public and private schools. Because charter schools are publicly funded, their teachers are technically considered public school teachers.

Nevertheless, eligibility for participation in the state retirement system, which is available to the majority of public school teachers, varies significantly from state to state. Most states allow charter school teachers to participate in the state teacher retirement system. And teachers in charter schools authorized by local public-school boards may usually participate. However, charter schools that are authorized by other entities, such as universities, municipalities, or other organizations may not be permitted to participate.

9.3   Private School Teachers

Private school teaching can offer advantages over teaching in a public school. Typically, private schools have smaller class sizes. Teachers might not have to deal with the same sort of bureaucracy that many public school teachers face. Some private school teachers may find it fulfilling to work in a school whose mission aligns with their religious or other beliefs. As an added bonus, the children of private school teachers may be offered tuition discounts if they attend the school where their parents teach.

A downside of teaching in a private school is that compensation is often less than in a public school. Compounding this problem is that there is no opportunity to participate in the state teacher retirement program. However, most private schools offer their teachers a retirement plan, which in most cases is a 403(b) plan. Some may even match teacher contributions up to 6 or 7%. As a result, in cases where a state has seriously underfunded the teacher retirement system, private school teachers in that state may enjoy better retirement plan benefits than public school teachers.

9.4   Tax Advantaged Retirement Accounts: 403(b) Plans

It's essential to understand the types of retirement plans that are available to you, and how you can use them to start building wealth.

Teachers in traditional public schools, charter schools, and private schools should generally be eligible to contribute to a 403(b) plan, which is a defined contribution (DC) plan. A 403(b) plan lets you contribute pretax dollars from your salary to a retirement investment account. That means the money you contribute each year is not taxed at the state or federal level, which effectively lowers your taxable income for that year. In addition, any earnings on the investments in your account accumulate on a tax-deferred basis, so you owe no tax on them until you eventually withdraw the money. The longer your money is invested, the more your account has the chance to grow in value. You also benefit from compounding.

Once you're enrolled in a 403(b) plan, the money you contribute is automatically deducted from your paycheck. You don't see that amount in your paycheck and, as many teachers have noted, "If you don't have it, you won't spend it." Once you get started, it seems painless.

Now, you might be thinking, there is no way you can afford to have your take-home pay reduced. If that's the case, one approach is to start contributing on a very small scale. Even 1% is better than nothing, and there are very few people who cannot get by on 1% less income. Contribute as much as you think you can.

If the school provides matching contributions to your plan, try to contribute at least enough to get the full match. That way, you are not passing up money that could be building your account. You may find it helpful, if you receive a modest pay raise in one year, to simply increase your contribution by the amount of that raise. If you do, you'll be taking home the same amount of money while increasing your savings. Over the years you can steadily increase your contribution until you reach the maximum permitted by the IRS.

Tax-deferred is not the same thing as tax-free. Eventually, you will need to pay federal taxes on the money you have socked away in your 403(b) plan. The tax you'll owe will be at the same rate that you'll be paying on your ordinary income. For most teachers, though, it's likely that you will be in a lower income tax bracket when you retire, reducing the amount you'll have to pay when you withdraw money from the plan. In most cases, you need to be at least 59 ½ to withdraw without owing a penalty. And you will have to start taking out Required Minimum Distributions (RMDs) starting at age 70 ½, unless you are still teaching at the same school.

If these details seem overwhelming, remember that you can and should get assistance from a representative at the financial firm that will manage your 403(b) account. Your school district might have a list of approved firms from which you can choose. Get to know your representative and plan to meet at least once a year to assess your current situation. Retirement accounts, like other investment portfolios, often need to be rebalanced periodically based on changes in the market, your risk tolerance, and how close you are to retirement age.

9.5 Tax Advantaged Retirement Accounts: Individual Retirement Accounts

Individual Retirement Accounts (IRAs) are personal retirement plans that are not offered through your employer or the government. Rather, you set up the account directly with the custodian, which may be a bank or brokerage firm, a mutual fund company, or another financial institution. IRAs are self-directed, meaning that you decide which investments to make. These can include stocks, funds, and bank products, as long as they are offered by the custodian of your account.

IRAs can be a powerful way to build your retirement savings because they grow tax-deferred, they offer extensive investment options, and their management fees are usually reasonable.

9.5.1 Traditional IRA

With a traditional IRA, your contributions grow tax-deferred, and taxes on any earnings are not due until you start making withdrawals. As of 2019, you can contribute up to $6000 of your earned income if you are under 50 and $7000 if you're over 50 in tax year 2019. That additional $1000 is referred to as a catch-up contribution. In addition, you can normally set up a spousal IRA under the same terms for a spouse who is not working.

As with other retirement plans, withdrawals cannot usually be made without a 10% penalty before you are at least 59½, but must be made as Required Minimum Withdrawals (RMDs) once you turn 70 ½. The amounts you withdraw are taxed at your regular tax rate.

9.5.2 Roth IRA

A Roth IRA shares some features with a traditional IRA: Both are self-directed and both let you make an annual contribution from earned income of $6000 per year, or $7000 per year if you are age 50 or older.

But there are differences between Roth and traditional IRAs;

- Contributions to a Roth IRA are paid for with after-tax dollars.
- Withdrawals taken from a Roth IRA are tax free, as long as you are at least 59 ½ years old, and the plan has been in existence for at least 5 years.
- Roth IRAs are not subject to RMDs, which means if you don't need the money, you can leave it in the account to continue to grow on a tax-free basis.
- There are income limits on how much you can contribute to a Roth. If your income is too high, you may not qualify for a Roth at all.

9.6 Self-Employed Retirement Saving

If you supplement your teaching income with work that you do as your own employer or as the owner of a small business, you may want to look into a Simplified Employee Pension, or SEP. These plans can provide you with another way to contribute toward your retirement in your role as a business owner or freelancer. If your small business has employees, they can participate in the SEP as well. SEPs resemble 403(b) plans, in that you and your employees (if you have them) can contribute to the plan on a tax-advantaged basis. You can set up the plan with a mutual fund company, brokerage firm, insurance company, or another financial institution.

9.7 Contributing to Multiple Accounts

If you have multiple retirement accounts – most likely a 403(b) plan and an IRA or Roth IRA, you'll have to decide how to allocate your savings across those accounts. If your employer matches your contributions, it makes sense to contribute enough to that account to make sure you get the highest possible matching contributions. Then, any retirement savings money that you have left over may be contributed to an IRA, Roth IRA, or SEP, depending on the amounts and sources of your income.

9.8 Asset Allocation

In both taxable investment accounts and tax-advantaged retirement portfolios, it's important to invest in an array of different types of investments. What percentage you decide to invest in each of the types is called asset allocation.

The thing to remember about asset allocation is that you can't just do it once when you enroll in a retirement account, and then forget about it. To maximize the potential for growth of your account value, and to minimize risk, especially when you are approaching retirement age and need to preserve the value of what you've accumulated over the years, you need to reallocate on a regular basis.

As a rule of thumb, you write down your age, put a percentage sign after it, and then invest that percentage of your portfolio in relatively less risky investments, like bonds. For example, a 40-year-old teacher would invest 40% of his or her portfolio in bonds. The other 60% would be in stock mutual funds, to take advantage of the possibility for strong returns and growth over the approximately 20 years remaining until retirement. Remember, stocks are regarded as a higher risk investment but historically are unlikely to lose money over a 20-year period. However, since people are living longer and their retirement funds need to last longer as well, some experts suggest that 10–20% more of your portfolio is allocated to stocks, making that allocation as high as 80%.

As you get older and closer to retirement, your portfolio should gradually shift towards an asset allocation that is less risky. That generally means more bonds and fewer stocks. This helps protect assets that have already accumulated value and reduce the impact of potential losses when your portfolio won't have as much time to recover.

If the thought of managing the shift in your portfolio allocation is intimidating, you might investigate life cycle funds, also known as target date funds. These mutual funds automatically adjust your allocation over time, to account for your increasing age and proximity to retirement. Specifically, the fund shifts the allocation from an emphasis on growth investments, like stocks, to more emphasis on less risky investments – bonds. The funds are timed to be keyed to different estimated retirement dates and are named that way. If, for example, you plan to retire around the year 2040, you would choose a fund with a 2040 target date. In addition to helping you manage risk while allowing for growth, these funds offer the added benefit of being already diversified.

9.9   Teacher Tipsheet: Retirement for Private and Charter School Teachers

- The federal government has designed tax advantaged retirement savings plans to provide incentives to save more.

- Having a 403(b) plan can help teachers in all situations but it is most important for private school teachers and for some charter school teachers who may not be able to rely on a state retirement plan.
- Contribute as much as you can to your 403(b) but be sure to contribute enough to receive any matching funds provided by your employer.
- IRAs are tax-advantaged plans that give you more control over your investments. The traditional IRA and the Roth IRA share several characteristics.
- A Roth IRA provides the advantage of having no required minimum.

9.10   Q&A

1. Can I dip into my 403(b) account if I have a financial emergency?
   - Yes, but it will cost you. If you withdraw money from a retirement account before age 59½, you may incur a 10% tax penalty, plus any additional penalties your state might assess. The penalties are on top of the regular income tax you'll have to pay on the amount that was withdrawn.
   - Your plan might allow you to borrow without incurring a penalty but the money will still need to be repaid.
   - In order to protect your retirement savings, it is important to set up an emergency fund. This is income, ideally 3–6 months' worth, that you set aside for unexpected expenses such as medical bills or a loss of income.
   - A Roth IRA can actually be used as a supplement to your emergency fund. Once you have 3 months' income set aside for a minor emergency, putting additional contributions into a Roth IRA can help you guard against a major emergency. If you depleted your regular emergency fund and had to withdraw from your Roth IRA, you could take out the originally invested money with no tax consequences—even if you had not reached age 59. And if you did not have a major emergency, you could just leave the extra saved money alone so it could continue to grow. This is in contrast to 403(b)s and traditional IRA accounts, which are not suitable for use as an emergency fund because of the penalties and taxes for early withdrawals.
2. I never enrolled in a 403(b) plan. Is it too late to sign up?
   - No. Now is the time to start. Make an appointment with the appropriate person in your human resources department. Let him or her explain your options to you. Then decide how much you can contribute during

each pay period. If you are age 50 or older, you are allowed to contribute more to your plan. Keep increasing your contribution each year until you reach the maximum the government will let you contribute.

3. How do I open a Roth IRA?
   – First, you need to make sure that you qualify. If you are single, you must have a modified adjusted gross income under $137,000 to contribute to a Roth IRA for the 2019 tax year, but contributions are reduced starting at $122,000. If you are married filing jointly, your modified adjusted gross income must be less than $203,000, with reductions beginning at $193,000.
   – Second, select a financial firm, such as a bank, mutual fund company, or insurance company to be the custodian for your Roth IRA. Look for companies that have low fees, good services, and a variety of investment options.

9.11   Financial 911 for Teachers

While financial emergencies like an unexpected medical bill or losing a job are undoubtedly serious, neglecting to save for retirement is perhaps the most significant. Without saving and investing for retirement, there will be no way to ensure that you will have enough money to live comfortably after you stop working. Once you are not earning an income, you will need the cash flow that retirement accounts can provide.

While teachers who can participate in a well-funded state retirement program have a certain level of financial security, it's essential for most charter school and private school teachers to proactively contribute to a defined contribution plan, including a 403(b), an IRA, or a SEP. The key is to let these accounts continue to grow, without withdrawing funds too early.

10

The Higher Education Connection

10.1 Teacher Case Study: Margaret Wonders What Went Wrong

Margaret stared at her student loan statements and wondered how she would ever pay off all that debt in her lifetime. Margaret had unexpectedly gotten into a doctoral history program after her first job out of college as a high school history teacher. Part-time work at her local university's history department, where she met faculty and graduate students, gave her the bug to go for a Ph.D. herself.

Where did she go wrong? Margaret stared at her student loan statements and wondered how she would ever pay off all that debt in her lifetime. Margaret had unexpectedly gotten into a doctoral history program after her first job out of college as a high school history teacher. Part-time work at her local university's history department, where she met faculty and graduate students, gave her the bug to go for a Ph.D. herself.

Margaret was off to a promising start, as she had gained college-level teaching experience while completing her history Ph.D. She was a teaching assistant for two undergraduate United States history survey courses. She developed her presentational, small-group discussion, and advising skills. Her doctoral advisor made sure that she presented papers at two national conferences. She also managed to get two articles published in national, peer-reviewed American history journals.

But, the job market for Ph.D. historians was discouraging when she started looking for a full-time job in higher education. She was prepared to accept

© The Editor(s) (if applicable) and The Author(s), under exclusive license to Springer Nature Switzerland AG 2021
T. Hunt Ferrarini et al., *Teachers Can Be Financially Fit*,
https://doi.org/10.1007/978-3-030-49356-1_10

modest pay in exchange for the academic lifestyle and tenure. As it turned out, she only could find temporary and visiting positions. Then she realized she was not even making as much money as her old high school teacher's salary!

And then there was the student debt. Margaret graduated with $40,000 in loans. Her first two years as a visiting professor were productive and provided good teaching and research experience. Margaret hadn't factored in the changes in higher education sweeping the field even as she was trying to start an academic career.

Margaret wasn't making much progress paying down her student loan debt. When her next job was only part-time, she cut back to only paying the amount labeled in her student loan papers as "forbearance." It was enough to keep her out of credit trouble but not enough to reduce the loan balance. With every month that went by, in fact, her student loan balance was growing. What advice could we give Margaret at this difficult point in her career?

10.2   Paying Down Student Loan Debt

Margaret is not alone in terms of having a large amount of student loan debt. Outstanding student loan debt reached an all-time high of $1.41 trillion in 2019. College tuition is a big factor in student loan debt, with out-of-state tuition and fees averaging $26,290 per year for a four-year public university and $35,830 for a private college. The average student loan balance per borrower hit a record high in 2018 of $35,359.

How can Margaret successfully pay off her student loans? The first thing to remember is that, as with other forms of debt, there is no silver bullet. However, some strategies are likely to be more successful than others. Paying off student loans will take time, discipline, and sacrifice.

10.2.1   How Much Do You Owe?

The first step is to figure out how much you owe. Most students have several loans so knowing how much you owe may not be obvious. To help you figure out what you owe, we suggest that you create a spreadsheet like the one in Table 10.1. (The APR is the Annual Percentage Rate. It is the interest rate for the whole year. It allows you to make easy comparisons.)

Table 10.1 How much student loan debt do you owe?

Lender	Loan amt	Balance	Payment	Term	APR
Lender 1	$20,000	$18,000	$185.00	10	4.0%
Lender 2	$10,000	$ 9000	$ 94.00	10	4.5%
Lender 3	$10,000	$ 7500	$ 84.00	10	6.0%
Total	$40,000	$34,500	$363.00		

10.2.2 Repayment Plan

Now that you know what you owe, let's come up with a repayment plan. There are two strategies to consider:

1. First, pay off the loans with the highest interest rates first. So, if you have one loan that is at 7% interest and another at 5%, pay the 7% off first. You will save money on interest payments because you'll first be paying down the loans that add the most interest each month. Then pay off the loan with the next highest interest rate, and so on until all loans are paid off.
2. The second approach is to pay off the loans with the smallest balance first. Here, you make minimum payments on all of your loans except for the smallest one. Prepay the smallest one as fast as possible. When that is accomplished, move onto the next biggest one. Continue until all loans are paid off.

Either of these approaches can make sense depending on the amounts involved and your personal preferences. Mathematically, if you pay off high-interest loans first you'll save more money – but psychology may work in your favor if you instead pay off small-balance loans first. Paying smaller-balance loans off first is the strategy we prefer because we think it builds confidence. That positive reinforcement of totally extinguishing that smallest-balance loan fortifies you to take on the next lowest loan. Table 10.1 represents Margaret's situation. For her, the repayment decision is easy because the highest APR is also the lowest amount owed. She should start paying down Lender 3.

10.2.3 Pay More Than the Minimum

The next strategy is to pay more than the minimum payment. You've probably heard this one before. If you're only paying the minimum payment each month, you're not getting to your goal very fast. You might not even be breaking even with the interest you're piling up. If you're paying only the "forbearance" amount, you're almost certainly not keeping up with interest.

By making larger payments, you'll be able to attack the amount you owe at a quicker rate. Here you are not just paying interest; you are reducing the principal. How to do that? Here's a suggestion: Whenever you have some unexpected income, apply it to the loan you are trying to pay off first. Think about cash gifts, tax returns, compensation for writing a book review, or giving a speech. How about using that income from teaching an overload course or a summer course to help pay down student loan debt?

10.2.4   Refinancing

The final strategy to consider is refinancing your student loans. To qualify for student loan refinancing, you'll need a good job like Margaret and good credit score. When you refinance, your new lender offers you a new loan at a lower interest rate and perhaps a shorter time frame to pay off the loan. The new lender pays off your existing loans. The lower interest rate reduces your monthly payment making it easier to pay the loan off. A word of caution: Government-funded student loans have certain protections and may offer alternative repayment schedules. Many have fixed interest rates. If you refinance a government loan with a private lender, you'll likely face interest rates that vary with the economy and little flexibility in repayment. Be sure you know what you're getting into in any refinancing.

Paying off student loans debt is doable. But, let's come back to earth for a minute. It is very possible that you are having trouble even making the minimum payments each month. What to do now? Remember, there is no silver bullet to get out of debt. We explained in Chap. 2 that everything starts with a budget. A budget helps organize your finances, track your spending and savings, and evaluate your overall financial health. For most people the steps are figuring out how to reduce spending, live below your means, and start reducing debt.

10.3   The Economics of Tenure

As Margaret wishes she had known sooner, higher education is changing. College professors used to face a stable career of middle-class incomes with little risk. No more. The incomes are highly variable across fields, locations, and types of institutions such as two year schools, four year schools, and research institutions (Table 10.2).

Table 10.2 Salaries for all new assistant professors (HigherEdJobs 2020)

Job title	Salary for all new assistant professors
Business, management, marketing, and related support services	$122,164
Communication, journalism, and related programs	$63,930
Computer and information sciences and support services	$95,000
Education	$62,000
Engineering	$90,167
English language and literature/letters	$62,000
Liberal arts and sciences, general studies, and humanities	$63,000
Mathematics and statistics	$72,999
Social sciences	$69,999

Even as incomes are more variable in higher education, job security is less. The American Association of University Professors reports that, at all U.S. institutions combined, 73% of higher education positions do not lead to permanent employment – that is, they are not on the "tenure track." These include adjuncts, postdocs, teaching assistants, non-tenure-track faculty, clinical faculty, and lecturers. For the most part, these positions have less job security than tenure-track positions. These folks sometimes cobble together part-time positions in order to make ends meet – something Margaret is now considering. Decreasing enrollments in higher education can also squeeze compensation for faculty.

10.3.1 Arguments for Tenure

Why, until recently, was tenure so widespread in higher education? The main argument is that tenure protects academic freedom. The reasoning is that having a life-time job leaves college and university faculty free to pursue new ideas, methods, and theories that may or may not be widely accepted. The fear is that without tenure protection research that cuts against the grain of mainstream thinking might never see the light of day.

The second argument for tenure is economic. Economic theory suggests that offering tenure allows colleges and universities to recruit and retain highly trained and skilled faculty while paying less than what non-academic employers do for employees with similar training and skills. This is called a "compensating differential." For example, if a job applicant is considering a job that is in an undesirable location or comes with other burdens, then the expectation is that the applicant will be offered higher pay as compensation for the sacrifice. Similarly, an individual with a newly minted doctorate might be willing accept something less in compensation in return for an offer of job security that is promised by earning tenure. Fringe benefits like great health insurance plans might also be used to offset the wage differential.

Tenure does not mean that professors cannot be released. If your college or university closes or downsizes because of financial distress, you may be out of a job even if you have tenure. Given the smaller student enrollments and other challenges predicted in the future, the prospect is more likely today than in earlier years.

Even if a college or university does not face financial distress, tenured professors can be and have been fired. However, the college or university has to show that the professor is incompetent or not performing required job assignments. Firing a tenured, full professor is likely to be a long, drawn out, and expensive process, so administrators in higher education only attempt a firing in the most extreme cases.

10.3.2   Arguments Against Tenure

Why are many institutions abandoning tenure? Most heads of colleges and universities believe that they have to be nimbler in order to compete for new students. If they have large numbers of tenured faculty, they're unable to respond quickly when students look to study in hot new areas such as STEM (science, technology, engineering, and mathematics). Instead the schools have to keep employing and paying tenured faculty in less sought-out disciplines.

The critics of tenure say that tenure limits the power of the administration to innovate with new courses, technology, and majors and certifications. Critics argue that tenure can be replaced by rolling, multi-year contracts similar to those in the private sector. They reason that professors who are good at what they do should have no problem. Professors who are not so good at what they do may be asked to move on. The critics argue further that multi-year, rolling contracts are also an effective means of protecting academic freedom.

Even if we acknowledge that compensating differentials may have operated in the past, most higher education administrators think that they can save money and be more efficient if they abandon tenure. Many of their faculty members understandably disagree.

So, what should someone considering a career in higher education do? To be successful, new graduate degree holders need to be more flexible than in past. Depending on the needs of the institution, they may need to demonstrate stronger teaching and writing skills. Publication in good journals and great teaching evaluations can help. Researchers may be expected to support their research through grants. Successful grant writing is very attractive to potential college and university employers.

Another way that new Ph.D. students can distinguish themselves is by earning online badges. Opportunities to earn online badges are proliferating. They can show evidence that a job applicant has acquired key skills in addition to their academic specialties. So, a history major might benefit from also having a badge in web development and design. A philosophy major might add value by having a badge in artificial intelligence. A mathematics major might benefit by earning a badge in social networking.

10.4   Retirement Planning

The retirement options for higher education faculty are similar to those that are available to K-12 faculty. We suggest that you read Chaps. 8 and 9 for more details. Here is a quick overview.

- Like K-12 teachers, many higher education faculty members participate in state teacher retirement programs. A state pension can be a great benefit. However, the sustainability of such programs varies from state to state. And, since they are all different, there are many decisions that will need to be made.
- If you have paid into Social Security, you will have to make many decisions as you approach retirement. Visit the Social Security Administration (http://ssa.gov) and set up an account. You can review your earnings history and use the calculators to get a clearer picture regarding your Social Security income in retirement.
- Be sure to take advantage of tax advantaged retirement accounts. These include 403(b) plans, Individual Retirement Accounts, and Simplified Employee Pension (SEP) accounts.

A financial institution called TIAA may be unfamiliar to K-12 educators, but is the largest financial institution specializing in providing financial services to college and university faculty. TIAA serves faculty in public as well as private institutions. It offers a variety of financial products including retirement annuities, IRAs, mutual funds, brokerage accounts, and so forth. It also has some good calculators and other financial planning tools. Since this financial institution is so widely recognized in higher education, it might be a good idea to visit it at https://www.tiaa.org/public

There are, however, many financial institutions that offer good returns and low fees. Whenever possible, it is better to shop around.

What of Margaret, whose story opened this chapter? Seemingly stuck as an "academic wanderer," she maintained her flexibility to move while continuing to offer high-quality classes and keep up with research in her area of history. After another year, this combination landed her a full-time job with benefits at a regional state university. By budgeting and earning extra income, she began to make progress whittling down her student loan balances.

In an appointment with her new employer's human resources department, Margaret set up automatic retirement savings with TIAA, then remembered that she already had a TIAA account from her visiting professorship right out of graduate school. (She had been receiving statements all along from that account but just ignored them.) Margaret was pleasantly surprised by how much her balances had grown and she looked forward to doing more about retirement as time went by. But most importantly, she was doing a job she loved – and although she never would have said so at the time, it was worth spending a few years trying to land a full-time continuing job.

10.5 Opportunities for Earning More Income

Higher education faculty like Margaret often encounter opportunities to earn income that are rarely available to K-12 teachers. Teaching schedules in higher education tend to be more flexible than at the K-12 level. Depending on the culture and policies of the institution, this flexibility can offer opportunities. College professors are more likely to be paid to travel to conferences, teach summer courses, teach overloads, give guest lectures, write books, do paid research, and provide consulting in their field. Some of these opportunities can be lucrative.

Whatever the difference in opportunities, the path to financial security for college-level educators is the same as for anyone else: start saving early, buy and hold stocks for the long-term, and diversify.

An old bromide for new college or university faculty is that "you have to learn how to say no." The idea of saying "no," of course, is for a new professor to avoid becoming overwhelmed with too many obligations. Some of those obligations might distract them from the task at hand – doing what needs to be done to earn tenure or contract renewal.

We disagree with the automatic "no." When you say "no," you are not just closing the door on one opportunity. You are potentially closing the door on many future opportunities. Successful consulting is often about building relationships over the long term. Building relationships often starts with a small project or two and later on may begin to develop into a lot more.

We suggest that you say "yes" when opportunities come your way assuming, of course, that you have the necessary expertise and wish to be associated with the organization or individuals who are making the offer. Besides, not every gig that comes your way will pan out. Even saying "yes" can lead nowhere. People fail to follow up. Dates don't work out. Plans change. Grants are not funded. Book deals are rejected. And so forth.

Some in popular culture portray college and university faculty jobs as a lazy path to easy street, with little actual work and big compensation. That portrayal is wrong. However, with the right effort, an academic career can be rewarding. Professors can be millionaires, too.

10.6 Teacher Tipsheet: Suggestions Regarding Consulting Income

- Be alert to opportunity. Small jobs like book reviewing or even giving free talks can lead to larger opportunities down the road.
- Be careful to track your income. Not all clients send you a 1099 form but they may have reported your income to the IRS. Record keeping is important.
- Be sure to set some of your consulting aside to pay income taxes. Most clients do not deduct taxes from your compensation so you are responsible for paying income taxes on your consulting income.
- As a consultant, you are running a small business. There are a series of decisions you need to make including whether to get an employer tax identification number and if you wish to establish an individual liability corporation, be a sole proprietor, or choose some other organizational alternative.
- As a small business, you can make contributions to a Simplified Employee Pension (SEP). This is potentially a great option for you. It is explained more fully in Chap. 8.
- What should you charge in fees? Obviously, that depends on many factors. How many hours are involved? Is travel involved or can you work from home? Does the client cover travel expenses? Our best advice is to ask other

people in your field about the fees they charge. Also, it is wise to stay somewhat flexible. You don't want to price yourself out of the market especially when you are just starting out. (For one of the authors, the first compensation for a writing project was a Wheaties sweatshirt.)

10.7   Q&A

1. Aren't there student loan forgiveness programs for folks in higher education?
   - Yes. There are programs that offer student loan forgiveness if you work long enough at an eligible public sector job. Professors at public state colleges or city colleges might satisfy the requirements for Public Service Loan Forgiveness (PSLF). To qualify for PSLF student loan forgiveness for professors, you'll need to work at least 30 h a week. Adjunct faculty might also be eligible. Check out PSLF by following this link: https://studentaid.gov/manage-loans/forgiveness-cancellation/public-service#qualifying-employment
2. I have been looking for a tenure track position for 5 years. Should I give up on one day having a tenured position?
   - Yes. Higher education is changing. While tenure-track positions still seem to be the gold standard, they do come with downsides. Tenure does not have a great reputation with the public. Anyone who went to college has encountered professors who were lousy teachers and yet had strong job protection. Great teachers and researchers often take pride in not having tenure. The roll-over contract offered to lecturers and holders of clinical professorships provide some job security and often have a clause offering tenure-like academic freedom protection. It is not all sweetness and light. Some faculty might consider you a second-class citizen. But, if you love to teach and your students love you back, who cares?
3. Do some colleges and universities frown on earning outside income?
   - You bet! Let's be really clear. Your primary obligation is to your college or university. The first order of business if you are starting a consulting business is to read the rules in the handbook of your institution and follow up by meeting with your dean, department chair, or other supervisor. Even so, many institutions are okay with consulting opportunities. Writing books, giving speeches, and doing research often enhances the reputation of the institution. Just be sure you follow all of the rules which might include reporting your sources and amount of income to the university or getting permission when a gig will take you away from campus.

10.8   Financial 911 for Teachers

If you have reached mid-career in any field but do not have retirement savings started, you have a financial 911. This can happen to some in higher education because they have had a succession of temporary or part-time appointments, but none with retirement benefits.

Some higher education faculty, regardless of their financial situation, do not think at all of retiring. They imagine that they will leave the classroom boots first. They really have no plan to retire. It's easy to do. Higher education offers many advantages. If you get satisfaction from teaching and writing and enjoy being independent, higher education can be great. Moreover, it is not physically demanding so continuing beyond normal retirement ages is not out of the question. All this might lull college professors into saving less than they should for retirement, even as others who would like to save find their circumstances don't permit it.

Our advice is: Save more for retirement. In our experience there are many who regret saving less but very few who regret saving more. This "asymmetric regret," as economists call it, makes it important to save, perhaps, more than you think you should.

Regarding academic retirement in general: If you are in your 30s or 40s, it is nearly impossible to know how you will feel in your 60s. Decades of grading papers, giving lectures, attending faculty meetings, serving on committees, writing grants, and going to conferences can, believe or not, get a little stale. You might wish to retire at age 65 but you may not have planned well.

Whether you have a little or a lot saved for retirement, we recommend that you take full advantage of all of the tax advantaged options that are available to you. Understand your state pension program or other defined benefit programs, if you have them. Know where you stand with Social Security. That way, you should have sufficient savings so that you can retire early if you wish. If you decide to teach for a few more years, all the better, assuming you're physically and mentally up for it.

But if you're at mid-career with little saved for retirement, it's time to sound the financial alarm and get going.

Reference

HigherEdJobs (2020) State College, PA. https://www.higheredjobs.com/salary/salaryDisplay.cfm?SurveyID=51. Accessed 2 April 2020.

11

Educators and Insurance

11.1 Teacher Case Study: Doing Everything Right and Getting It Wrong

Jayden and Alyssa prided themselves on doing insurance right. Jayden's grandfather had been in the insurance business and he always reminded them about being covered. They fully insured everything they could think of, getting:

- Coverage on their cars through a national insurer with extensive advertising (reassuring them every time they saw their insurance company on a football game commercial).
- Complete homeowners' coverage from their car insurance agent, who was happy to add the homeowners' coverage at a discount.
- A thorough life insurance package that would insure both of them, build cash value, and never be revoked as long as they paid the premiums, also sold through their car insurance agent.
- Complete health insurance coverage at work with vision and dental as well as low deductibles and copays.

The coverage came in handy, paying for everything from a cracked car windshield to their kids' braces. Jayden and Alyssa did everything right, from the viewpoint of their insurance agent – always choosing more coverage and more complete coverage. And yet, even without any uninsured disasters, they ended up with dramatically less wealth because of their insurance choices. How could that be? This chapter shows how "good insurance choices" often

© The Editor(s) (if applicable) and The Author(s), under exclusive license to Springer Nature Switzerland AG 2021
T. Hunt Ferrarini et al., *Teachers Can Be Financially Fit*,
https://doi.org/10.1007/978-3-030-49356-1_11

mean less complete coverage. To understand why, we have to start with the nature of risk and insurance.

11.2   Risk and Insurance

Insurance experts say there is risk in everything, but is it true in all these cases?

- You get coffee at a fast-food drive-through.
- You send a text to your friend during a dull professional development session.
- You go for a bike ride in your neighborhood.

The answer is "yes," there is risk in all three. The coffee from the drive-through might spill and burn you. If you send a text to a friend during that dull session, you may get a big frown from an administrator and consequences later. If you ride your bike safely, there's still a chance that you could be struck by a car or hit a bad utility grate. Even if you stayed in bed to avoid all these risks, you would increase your health risk from being inactive! We have to conclude that there is risk in everything – but we can manage it in a variety of ways.

Insurance is a common way of dealing with risk. There are others. To understand the options, let's take a trip back in time to the early days of health insurance, which history tells us happened in the 1920s in the U.S.

11.2.1   How to Manage Risk

Let's take the example of the Old Town School District, which in 1926 has 100 teachers and is ahead of its time on matters of health. There is always the possibility that one of the teachers will require treatment in Old Town Hospital. In advance no one knows who it will be. One day the education association, forerunner of a later union, has a meeting to consider how to handle the risk. There are many ideas, but they all come down to three basic options:

1. Assume the risk
2. Reduce the risk
3. Share the risk

Assuming the risk is what's happening already (the default). If one of the teachers requires hospital treatment, tough. The hospitalized teacher and family somehow come up with the money. It is a good deal less in the 1920s than now but it still hurts. The strategy of assuming a risk, and just accepting it when it happens, is referred to as *self-insuring*.

The second option is to reduce the risk. The teachers of Old Town can, to the best of their ability, carefully avoid the conditions that might put them in the hospital. The best case is that none of the 100 will require hospital treatment. Yet the risk never really goes away, and in time almost everybody will need to go to the hospital.

The third option for the 100 teachers would be to share the risk. These teachers could make a deal: Each one agrees to contribute 1/100 of the average cost of a hospitalization. The teachers association now has the ability to cover that one hospitalization. Ideally, everyone contributes and no one has to bear the entire loss. Each member of the pool has an obligation to pay a 1/100 share of the treatment cost.

Those are the three options. Is insurance a fourth option beyond assuming the risk, reducing the risk and sharing the risk? Not really – insurance is just a way of sharing the risk. In this example, the teacher's association has implemented a simple form of insurance. In reality, such an arrangement would be difficult to manage. What if someone needed very expensive treatment? Would it be fair for the youngest teacher with great health and little risk to pay a large insurance bill calculated to cover an older pool? What if more than one member of the association needed treatment? Then the whole thing falls apart.

11.2.2 How Insurance Works

In yesteryear and today, a real-life Old Town Teachers Association would be far better served by working with an insurance company. The teachers would still be sharing risk and yet the sharing would be better administered. With insurance, the money to pay claims originates with the money paid by customers, known as premiums. It makes sense to draw from a large customer base beyond Old Town. Further, in the event that two or three or 10 teachers are hospitalized in a given year, having access to a larger pool of funds through an insurance company is a big help.

Even with a company acting as the organizer, insurance is still about a group of people sharing and managing risk. The checks that compensate you for insured losses are written by a company, so it's natural to say the money comes "from the company." However, it's worth remembering that the money passing through an insurance company originally came from the company's customers. Insurance is a way to enable people to share and manage risk, not a source of free money from beyond the sky.

Insurance today works through markets. If those markets function work well, customers get a good deal and the rates are reasonable. Every year, some people may feel that if they do not "use" their insurance, it is a waste of money. For example, someone pays homeowner's insurance premiums for a year, nothing goes wrong, and the money is considered wasted. Is that correct? No, the homeowner had the protection for a year, the protection was valuable, and the insurance was required by the mortgage lender. But how do you make good decisions on insurance?

11.3   Strategy for Good Insurance Decisions

The key strategy for good insurance decisions is to *manage large and uncertain losses* – such as a tree falling through your roof in a storm. It would take many thousands of dollars to clean up the damage, restore the structure and redo the interior. In contrast, small known costs should be handled without insurance. Homeowner's insurance does not cover the cost of replacing furnace filters, a small and known cost. Insuring the costs of replacing furnace filters would not be smart coverage, because of the expense of collecting the money up front, handling claims for filters and writing checks. The example may be far-fetched but the principle is important. If insurance covers a small known expense, it's not risk coverage at all, but rather just an expensive way of pre-paying for something.

It may seem odd, but with the best insurance strategies you will often pay in, rarely if ever getting anything back. To put it another way: *You do not want to collect*. Here are some reasons why:

- If you are going to collect, something bad such as a fire or accident must have happened.
- If you have a loss, insurance does not cover it all. Even when it covers the entire loss of money, you still have lost the time and trouble of following the claims procedures and taking care of the damage.
- When you buy insurance to cover small and certain costs, you're really just pre-paying.

All of this comes into play when you choose a *deductible* on your insurance coverage. The deductible is the amount you must pay before your insurance kicks in. When you have "first-dollar coverage" as Jayden and Alyssa preferred in our opening case study, you don't have to pay a deductible. However, that sort of coverage is expensive for the insurer and the customer.

A better strategy is to discipline yourself to save up an emergency fund to pay for what insurance does not cover – and then go for a higher deductible. You'll find that higher-deductible insurance is far less expensive. It is usually possible to save up more than enough to cover future losses. (Notice that this strategy depends on self-discipline. It's not smart to go for the big deductible without having some way of managing uncovered expenses in the event of a loss.)

Let's see how good insurance strategy looks in different areas.

11.3.1   Car Insurance

There are three main categories for risk that come from owning and driving a car: (1) the expense of repairing or replacing a car damaged in a *collision*; (2) the risk of *liability* to pay for damage that you caused; and (3) the risk of hazards such as fire, theft or storms, handled by *comprehensive* coverage.

In all these areas, a good strategy would involve reducing some risks and then assuming small risks by having a high deductible. You can resolve to drive carefully and lock the car when you leave it. But liability for risk is another matter. What if your accident on the Interstate totals a truckload of iPhones? State law will typically require liability coverage as a condition of your driving anyway.

When your car has gotten old and substantially less valuable, it will probably pay you to drop collision coverage and instead save your money toward replacing the car. In all these decisions you are not expecting to "fully insure" or to "get a lot of money back." Getting a lot of money back is what you're trying to avoid.

11.3.2   Insurance at Home

Whether you are a homeowner or a renter, you should consider your strategy for covering risks where you live. If you are a homeowner, homeowner's insurance is a good idea. It will cover most risks of damage and the huge risks that come from liability. If someone slips and falls on your sidewalk, later requiring a quarter million dollars' worth of hospital treatment, you're on the hook for that if you are not insured. Ordinarily you will be required to have homeowner's insurance because of your mortgage.

If you rent, you have a choice to make, since renter's insurance is typically not required. The coverage is inexpensive compared with the risks involved and so renter's insurance is a good idea.

Whether you rent or own, your strategy should again be to reduce some risks, by locking doors when you leave and maintaining smoke detectors. Small risks you should assume. The big risks such as fire, theft, and liability would be handled by insurance. If you save up an emergency fund to pay for uninsured losses, you can afford a high deductible that will greatly reduce your regular costs.

11.3.3   Life Insurance

When the owner of a life insurance policy dies, the policy pays a beneficiary. The policy actually insures your earning ability rather than your life. A 22-year-old starting teacher with no dependents has very little need for life insurance because no one is depending on that person's income.

Reducing risk in the case of life and earning ability is a good idea. It would include paying attention to your health and safety, such as by not smoking or always wearing a seat belt in a car. Given the realities of life and death, though, you're always assuming some risk. But for people whose income is important to others, sharing the risk through life insurance is a good idea. A mid-career teacher who is the main breadwinner in a family with children should certainly have life insurance. One good rule is to carry insurance equal to about ten times the breadwinner's annual income.

The kind of insurance that most efficiently provides a death benefit is called *term insurance*. The policyholder pays regular premiums and then if the policyholder dies, the policy pays specified dependents. This is called "term" life insurance because it lasts for a fixed term such as five or 10 or 30 years, possibly with a renewal option up to a certain age. For people with a need to insure income, term life insurance is overwhelmingly recommended by personal finance experts.

11.3.4   Health Insurance

No one is exempt from having a medical emergency, and medical care is expensive. This means that health insurance is important for all of us. Even a totally healthy person can get into an expensive accident. Health insurance is controversial because it is the subject of major political action in Congress and the courts.

Like other forms of insurance, health insurance typically makes only partial payments. There are separate names and definitions for amounts not paid by health insurance:

- As referred to in health insurance, the *deductible* is the annual amount you are responsible for before your coverage takes over. Someone with a $5000 deductible will generally have to pay for the first $5000 in health care expenses (with a few exceptions, like physicals provided without charge).
- The *copayment* or *copay* is the fee per doctor visit or prescription. Copays for doctor visits often fall in the $25 to $100 range but have become higher in recent years.
- Even after copayments and deductibles are met, most policies do not pay all of the rest. The percentage paid after copayments and deductibles are met is *coinsurance*. A common arrangement is that the insurance pays 80% and the policyholder pays 20% on the amounts that are subject to coinsurance.

Smart health insurance involves all three strategies: assuming, reducing, and sharing risk. You would want to assume small risks, such as paying for over-the-counter medications. You can reduce other risks with good health habits like diet and exercise. But no matter how healthy your lifestyle, insurance is typically required against the big expenses and accidents. You as a teacher may have a substantial advantage, in that most teachers have relatively good health insurance benefits. You may know some teachers who handle all of the health insurance for their families because their benefits are better than their spouses'. They put all their dependents on the school policy because its terms are better than those commonly available from private employers.

Health insurance involves more money and bigger risks than other kinds of insurance. It's important to consider carefully the tradeoff presented by a high deductible. The Bronze plans popularized by the Affordable Care Act have low premiums – but in return, they have high deductibles. You pay more out-of-pocket but you also have lower premiums. On the other hand, Silver and

Gold plans cost more each month but have smaller deductibles. If you can, try to predict upcoming medical expenses and decide accordingly. You can't know for sure but you can try to make a smart guess.

Whatever deductible you choose, comparing health insurance is a good idea. Because of large differences between premiums and coverage you can save a lot of money. Even if your school system offers only a small number of plans, it's worth comparing the ones you do have.

11.4   What Jayden and Alyssa Did Wrong

In our opening case study, Jayden and Alyssa seemed to do everything right. Their insurance decisions certainly made them better off than if they were under-insured or uninsured. Still, different insurance choices might have made them substantially wealthier. Here's what they did wrong:

- They stayed with a national insurer instead of shopping around for car coverage. Little did they know that, like many customers or national insurers, they were being penalized for their loyalty as their rates crept up over time. At any point after the first few years, they could have gotten a better deal by getting competing quotes (often from less well known but financially sound companies recommended by independent insurance agents). They missed out on thousands of dollars' worth of savings.
- They went for a low deductible and complete coverage. That was nice when the car windshield needed replacing—they didn't pay anything then—but had they gone for a higher deductible and saved the difference, they would have been thousands of dollars better off. Their "complete coverage" included things like roadside assistance they already had with their auto club, so they were paying for coverage they literally would never use. (They did not even know they had it.)
- They bought homeowners' insurance without shopping around. Even with discounts from having both policies with the same company, over time they paid thousands more than they would have from getting competing quotes. Like car insurance rates, those rates crept up over time, almost like a "loyalty penalty" rather than a "loyalty discount."
- They added vision and dental to their health coverage, but because these expenses are relatively predictable the coverage is costly. They could have come out better by saving up for those expenses.
- Worst of all, they bought whole-life insurance without understanding the benefits of term life insurance. Their "whole life" policy, as the name

implied, covered them for their whole lives – even after their kids would be grown and their need for life insurance coverage would be minimal. They had not heard what a bad deal most whole-life insurance is compared with term insurance.

Jared and Alyssa's other insurance decisions had tiny effects compared with the lost wealth they could have had with a better life insurance strategy. If they had gone for 30-year term life insurance and invested the money they saved by not buying whole life insurance, they would have been $200,000 richer! And the 30-year term would have covered all the years when insurance would have been most important.

Notice this one very important point: If Jayden and Alyssa had simply spent the money saved through term life insurance (instead of investing it), they would have been poorer. So if you think you won't invest the difference, whole life insurance might be right for you. Ask yourself: Can you discipline yourself if $200,000 is on the line? Answer realistically and act accordingly.

11.5   Conclusion: Getting a Good Deal

Whatever kind of insurance you're seeking, there are three general rules for getting a good deal:

1. Shop around. Even if you checked different insurers for your coverage in the last few years, large changes are possible. The best deal for you may have gotten a lot better in the meantime.
2. Don't forget that the main purpose of insurance is to protect against large and uncertain losses! It is costly and inefficient to insure against small known losses. If you pay attention to health and safety in your daily life, while keeping a good emergency fund available, you can also save by choosing high deductibles for your insurance coverage.
3. Be sure to reduce risks, as by maintaining a hazard-free home, checking smoke detectors regularly, and driving safely

We all understand that risk cannot be eliminated. But with a modest amount of care and effort, risk can be managed. The result will be lower risks of loss and potentially large savings of money.

11.6   Teacher Tipsheet on Insurance

- Understand that there is risk in everything. While you can manage it, you can't totally avoid it.
- Managing risk will involve a combination of assuming some risks, reducing others, and sharing still others.
- Insurance is a good way of sharing risk, but you need to make smart decisions.
- You can save a lot of money if you can discipline yourself to save up an emergency fund and then go for large deductibles on your insurance coverage.
- Term life insurance is far more cost-effective than whole life insurance for guarding against the loss of an earner's income.
- It is vital to have health insurance in today's world.

11.7   Q&A

1. Will I always be better off by following your advice?
   - Frankly, no. When it comes to risk, nothing is certain and we can only tell you what works most of the time. If you save up an emergency fund and choose high deductibles, you will generally come out better over a long period of time. The longer you follow the strategy, the more the numbers are in your favor. But you could still get a cracked windshield like Jayden in the first month of your strategy and be out $1000 right away. At that point, it would be small comfort that over the long run you'll be far better off. We sympathize but the numbers are what they are.
2. Why shouldn't I want insurance that pays me something back instead just always taking my money?
   - Insurance that is sure to pay you something back is insurance for a high-probability event. If it's almost certain to happen, then the insurance is more a form of prepayment than a form of risk coverage. But it's expensive prepayment because you have to cover the insurance company's costs of billing and collecting and paying claims, instead of just paying the amount yourself.

3. Why do I see even-handed comparisons of term life insurance and whole life insurance online if you say whole life insurance is so bad?
   - Let's try two answers, the first one more charitable to the industry. The life insurance industry recognizes you'll be far better off if you buy term life insurance and invest the difference. But if you don't invest the difference, you'll just have spent that money and the insurance will not have helped your wealth grow. Even though whole life insurance is less effective, it does cause wealth to grow over time. That's the first answer.
   - The second answer, less charitable to the industry, is that the industry makes far higher profits on whole life insurance. The commissions to those doing the selling are amazingly high. Your cash value builds very slowly. When a client has the ability to buy term and invest the difference, being sold whole life insurance amounts to transferring wealth from the insured to the selling agent.
   - Which explanation applies? We'll let you decide.
4. Should I buy long-term care insurance for future nursing home expenses?
   - This is a hard call even for very well-informed insurance consumers. Long-term care is itself expensive and therefore the premiums are also expensive. Long-term care insurance is not for the rich or for people of very modest means. The rich can just pay for long-term care from their assets as needed. People who don't have much money, on the other hand, have little choice other than to assume the risk (and then fall back on government programs like Medicaid when they have no assets remaining and need nursing care). In between the rich and those of modest means, there is a case for long-term care insurance to preserve assets if someone needs that care. Perhaps the best advice is, whatever your solution to long-term care, do not buy the coverage under pressure without shopping around. Full-service financial advisers who handle both insurance and investments will generally have more to offer you than someone who has insurance products only.

11.8 Financial 911 for Teachers

If you have lost health insurance coverage or are about to lose it, this is a financial 911. Even if you are in great health, an auto accident could easily put you in the hospital to the tune of $250,000 or $500,000 or more. Here are some facts to know about this emergency:

- If you lose coverage because you have lost your job, short-term coverage is available through something called COBRA. The COBRA law may let you pay to stay on your employer' health insurance plan. But it's only for a limited time after your job ends and you will probably find the coverage costly. Even so, it's better than going without if you can at all afford it.
- You may be eligible for health insurance through the Affordable Care Act exchanges, even outside of the annual open enrollment period. There's a special enrollment period for those who have lost jobs. Check healthcare. gov for details.
- You may only be able to afford a policy that covers catastrophic expenses and requires you to pay out-of-pocket for just about everything else. Even so, this is coverage worth having because it saves you from possible financial disaster.

If nothing works and you have no coverage at all, remember that you can still get treatment by paying cash. Doctors, especially solo practitioners, may be willing to offer a deal to get you the care you need. If all else fails and you have a medical emergency, go to the hospital for treatment. It will take a while to sort things out later, but no one wants you to suffer serious impairment or death for lack of insurance.

12

Unconventional Risk Management

12.1 Case Study: Penelope's Life Changes Suddenly

Bad things happen to good people. Penelope knows this well. One evening she turned on the nightly news and learned that her husband was in a fatal accident. Life for Penelope and their three-year-old son forever changed.

Penelope had been working part-time as a high school math teacher. Now, she had to step forward as the primary income earner. Her part-time income salary would not allow her and her son to live comfortably while saving regularly, preparing for her son's college years, investing for her retirement, or even financing a summer trip to see family.

An emergency savings account provided some cushion to sort things out. A will allowed Penelope to quickly sell her husband's car to rid her of his monthly car payments. Life insurance covered all burial expenses and paid off his student loans and credit card debt. Some funds were left over for their son's college education and her retirement. The house was sold and they moved in to an affordable rental unit within walking distance of her son's school. Gone were the heavy monthly mortgage payments and the worries of home maintenance.

On her new life path, Penelope eventually decide to relocate. She found a job in a small town close to relatives. After weighing all the positives against the negatives, she decided accepting a teaching contract at a remote school offering more job security as well as family support. These factors were more

© The Editor(s) (if applicable) and The Author(s), under exclusive license to Springer Nature Switzerland AG 2021
T. Hunt Ferrarini et al., *Teachers Can Be Financially Fit*,
https://doi.org/10.1007/978-3-030-49356-1_12

important to Penelope than staying at her current school in a bustling city with pending budget cuts.

Fast-forward, Penelope still teaches at the same school. Her son entered one of the military academies to do his undergraduate studies. Though Penelope did not plan to live any part of the life that actually materialized, she (and her son) found happiness. She gives partial credit to financial security provided by financial preparations and plans for living in a complex world that includes uncertainties.

12.2   Managing Unconventional Risks

In life, there is a wide range of unconventional risks. Disaster strikes when someone suddenly dies, your spouse unexpectedly loses a job, you face divorce, a child battles addiction, an outbreak of illness shuts down your city, or you get fired because of something posted on social media. The time to think about these unconventional risks is now – before disaster strikes. Put a plan in place to help navigate life during and after.

Unfortunately, unlike ordinary financial risks, these risks cannot be eliminated or protected against through the purchase of insurance. This gives some people reason to say that it is impossible to manage them. So, forget them. People like Penelope disagree. She and others like her advocate preparing for the unexpected. If your financial house is in order and you have contingency plans in place for income, saving, and spending, the extraordinary becomes slightly more manageable.

Unconventional risks make this the most difficult chapter of the book. Decide now to take them on. When events happen to disturb the center of your world and shake you at your core, the future payoffs will be immeasurable. Today's costs are minimal.

In a moment's notice you could be walking in Penelope's shoes for similar or different reasons. Consider following some guidelines. Doing so can help you and your loved ones sleep better at night knowing plans exist should something extraordinary and devastating happens.

12.3   Be Prepared

There are certain things you can do now so you are prepared just in case the unexpected does happen.

12.3.1 Place All Important Documents in One Place

Start with placing all important documents in one place that is both safe and relatively easy to access. They may be needed with little notice and won't do much good if they can't be found or are locked up somewhere inaccessible.

Gather your insurance policies, financial statements, tax returns, will, advanced directives (more on this below), and a list including all usernames and passwords for online accounts. Place everything in a safe place like a fire-proof safe or safe deposit box. Have relatively quick access to the location.

12.3.2 Have an Updated Will

Can you believe it? The pop star Prince was fighting an addiction, and he died at age 57 without a will. Legendary singer Aretha Franklin lost her brutal struggle with pancreatic cancer at 76, and she had no will.

Wow! Think about it. What does it mean for someone not to have a will? When someone dies without a will the estate of the deceased goes into pro-bate, and the state's laws and its judicial system take over whatever assets are in probate. A representative for the deceased is designated and is responsible for providing a full list of assets and liabilities of the deceased. A probate court determines legal heirs, designates what each receives in net assets (value of assets after all the liabilities are paid), and distributes what remains. The wishes of the deceased never enter the equation. Everything occurs based on state law, and probate fees and court costs are deducted from the net assets which can be problematic for small estates.

A will is a good idea even if you may have a small estate. Creating a will designates beneficiaries and identifies who gets what remains of your personal belongings, pets, and net assets. A will provides relief to those left behind and would have to take everything through probate. It also guarantees that you, not a probate court, determines how to distribute items those things of value especially those with special memories and family significance.

We understand. No one wants to think about dying. Unfortunately, every-one does. A will helps compartmentalize that part of your life and lays out what happens in the event of your death. This can be especially important when deciding the custody of minors, possessing investments specifically des-ignated to fund college, and so forth.

Creating a will has never been easier or less expensive. Hop online. Choose one that complies with your state laws. Answer a series of questions. The answers will give you time to think about how to distribute what remains of your estate (assets less liabilities) in the unlikely event of your death. Otherwise others in a probate system will make these decisions for you. Want to set up a trust fund for your offspring rather than giving cash to do whatever? State it. Name who gets your car, prized possessions, and family jewelry. Decide who cares for any pets (after receiving consent, of course.) This list goes on.

Once finished, follow instructions to comply with your state's laws about signing, notarizing and safekeeping of the documents. Make sure your original will is in a safe place and make sure there are copies with the rest of your other important documents.

In summary, wills are not just for the rich and famous. They are for people like Penelope and her husband – like you. Wills help minimize the stress of living in a world without you, and they clarify your last wishes.

12.3.3   Advance Directives

Talking about death is difficult. Discussing end-of-life medical care can be even more so. This is important because decisions must be made on your medical treatments and your finances. If you are not of sound mind and body, someone else must decide for you.

Advance directives cover these possibilities. They describe under what conditions you want to be connected to a feeding tube or ventilator. They can also name who gets medical and financial power of attorney (if you are not married) so someone else can make healthcare and financial decisions on your behalf when you cannot.

Different states have different laws regarding advance directives and power of attorney. Some states combine the two. Most states make it easy. They have written or online forms that are in compliance with state laws. They offer questions that take your answers and generate a printable document that is customized to represent you and your wishes. Once complete, print and notarize. Place this legal document in safekeeping with all other important documents. Also share copies with your power of attorney(s) and primary healthcare provider.

12.3.4   Insurance

Although you cannot insure against unconventional risks and unfortunate tragedies, you can keep your regular insurance in order—and that will help. Insurance may seem expensive, as discussed in Chap. 10, but it provides protection that can be worth its weight in gold when tragedy strikes. Numerous studies show insurance is worth it. Remember, everyone lives in an uncertain world and stuff just happens. Make sure you have the proper mix of life, health, disability, and property insurance for you and your life situation. Place all insurance policies with your important documents.

12.4 Plans to Manage Your Financial House When the Unexpected Happens

Now, let's talk about planning to deal with the risks that come along with unplanned dips in income, unexpected spikes in expenses, out-of-the-ordinary credit and debt problems, and the possibility of a significant drop in the value of key assets due to crises in the economy. You can't know in advance of the downside risks associated with your (1) income, (2) expenses, (3) credit and debt, and (4) big assets (house or retirement portfolio). Still, you can have a few things set in place to manage life when they happen.

The advice that follows is intended to place you and your loved ones in a better position to tackle unconventional problems than if you had no plans in place. The goal is to reduce stress and provide some "relief" during extraordinary times. When disaster strikes your situation will be unique. So, the following guidelines are intentionally basic but they are carefully connected to the advice given in previous chapters. The important thing to remember is that a simple plan is better than no plan when something bad happens to shake you at your core.

12.4.1 Income Risks

Income risks are associated with income shocks. An income shock occurs when you or a member of your household's ability to earn income is reduced or eliminated. For one or another reason, everyone will likely face a such a period during a lifetime. Prepare for yours.

The reasons for an income shock are varied. You could lose your job because of budget cuts or posting different things on social media. Penelope's spouse died. Many spouses lost jobs during the Great Recession of 2008. Still others lost them because of addiction or for health or disability reasons. Even with insurance, an expected loss of income for an unknown period of time can have rippling effects.

To prepare for these drops in income and give yourself time to regroup, consider adding cushion to your emergency savings account. Extend the amount of total savings reserved for unexpected disruptions in income from 3–6 months to 6–9 months.

Next, have a short list of ways you can supplement income. Revisit Chap. 3 and jot down some concrete ideas and pertinent information now.

Prepare for the possibility of unemployment and have a plan to follow should you find yourself suddenly laid off or fired. You will have to ramp up your income efforts in other ways. Here are three ways.

1. Do not waste any time in filing for unemployment insurance and know what to expect in your state. Benefits and the periods of eligibility vary across states. So does compliance. While some states permit teachers on unemployment to substitute and serve as classroom aides for a couple of days a week, others do not. Don't make a simple mistake and risk your state's unemployment program.
2. Update your resume and immediately begin a job search. Register online as a job seeker. Reach out to any potential employers with whom you have deep connections, find out where schools are hiring by working your professional networks, and go online to identify the schools with teacher shortages. Seek out school systems experiencing unusually big waves of retirement. Also find states reducing class size or expanding programs per pupil.
3. Remain professionally active and current. The labor market keeps moving when you are unemployed or underemployed. To keep abreast of key changes in the labor market, check out the Bureau of Labor Statistic's Occupational Outlook Handbook. It will provide a broad look at what is happening across the economy in the teaching field. Browse and identify other jobs that make use of the skill sets and experiences possessed by teachers. Consider them. To abreast of what is happening in your subject area or schools, join a teacher Facebook group, complete a master's class in education or your discipline, get a certificate, and present at conferences. Keeping your name out there will send a signal to others who will know that you are willing, able, and ready to be called into action any time.

12.4.2 Expense Risks

Expense risk involves more complexity than income risk. If expenses get too high, using credit and taking out loans are options—but you have to be very careful.

Like income shocks, expense risks are varied. A natural disaster sweeps away all that you own. A new, expensive drug is not covered by insurance but is needed by a family member. A child's team enters a championship and the entire family wants to go watch. A scammer can take out loans in your name which take time to sort out.

You can mobilize your emergency savings but should you, especially if it means depleting the account to zero? Or should you consider the use of strategic credit and debt? That answer depends, in part, on your debt-to-income (DTI) ratio.

One popular DTI ratio compares your total recurring debt and mortgage to your recurring income. It can help assess your comfort level with spikes in expenses and should be a big influencer in making your final decision to draw down savings or borrow through credit cards or loans. A low DTI provides a helpful cushion. It makes temporary withdrawals from emergency savings to finance spikes in expenses a good option. Plus, lenders with favorable terms and companies with flexible card balances will be attracted to you. The opposite holds if your DTI is high.

Know your DTI and keep it low. Consult with an expert on identifying a targeted DTI for you and your circumstance. Need help figuring out yours? Grab all the last monthly statements for all your loans and credit cards and head into your primary financial institution for assistance.

Mitigate expense risks by forming good spending habits, maintaining a low DTI ratio, and being mindful that the spending of today has consequences that lie in the future. When possible, control your expenses. Do not let them control you.

Numerous resources exist online to learn more about how people have turned their old spending habits into good habits. Over a lifetime, sensible, purposeful spending relieves financial stress and anxiety. Place your spending plan front and center in your budget for life. Commit to spending less than you earn while build a cushion for emergencies in your savings account. Should something unusual happen causing expenditures to rise, you are covered. Replenish your savings as soon as the situation has been addressed. And, above all, make sure that you're not using credit or borrowing to put off dealing with a persistent spending problem.

12.4.3 Credit and Debt Risks

Credit and debt risks involve the likelihood that your credit or debt situation is preventing you from reaching your financial goals. These risks can also be involuntary or voluntary.

Involuntary risks exist when someone steals your identify and uses it fraudulently. It may or may not involve a scam. Regardless, this type of activity can cause huge debt and credit problems. Protect yourself by regularly monitoring your credit reports, checking out suspicious activity on credit cards, and carefully looking over your billing statements. Immediately report any problems to the three credit bureaus. Though getting everything worked out on your credit reports may take time, financial institutions are usually quick to act and usually remedy the situation in your favor.

The standard advice you've probably heard on identify theft is take action to protect yourself. Use secure passwords. Never share them. Update them frequently. Never give out your Social Security number or account numbers to anyone other than trusted professionals working for you. If you don't protect your identity, the identity thieves and scammers can use your private information to claim your assets, charge on your credit cards, and deplete your checking or savings accounts. These are things that can increase stress in your life and negatively affect your credit history making it difficult to borrow at relatively low interest rates, find favorable loans, enter lease agreements, and get jobs.

Some credit and debt risks are voluntary. Some teachers report that their balances on credit cards are too high, they accepted too much in student loans without planning for repayment, and they entered mortgage agreements with big monthly payments. Given their income, this can leave them with a very high debt-to-income level. Each teacher's situation is different and personal. So are the situations of others. So, let's take look at what's happening nationally with debt.

According to the Federal Reserve Bank of New York data, home mortgages account for the largest share of total personal debt in the U.S. Student loan debt takes on a distant second with credit card debt just falling behind. Some claim that historically high student loan debt is a heavier debt burden than either auto loans or credit cards. By bringing all these debt considerations together and comparing them with the average incomes earned in the teaching profession, could present a problem if some basic advice is not followed.

Determine your debt-to-income situation. Take steps based on it to improve your overall financial health. Calculate your total monthly debt load by summing all debt including car loans, home mortgage, credit card debt, student loan debt, and so forth. Position this total against your income total. "DTI calculators" are readily available online. Your bank likely has one, too. Take a look at yours and compare it to what the experts say it should be. In general, you will gain the most from carrying a low debt-to-income ratio. It will open you to the widest set of backup options when you find yourself in unforeseen situations and having to deviate from your master financial plan.

Should you discover that your DTI ratio is high, take action to lower it in order to improve your quality of life. Research shows that uncomfortably high DTIs hurt people at home as well as at the workplace. Put best practices and comprehensive strategies described on the internet into practice. Consult with an expert if you like. Check with your employer. A growing number of employers is offering to pay down student loans to relieve employees of personal debt and lift moral. The hope is that workplace wellness should improve. Over time, improvements in productivity should follow.

Bottom line. Align your credit and debt with your financial goals relative to your overall income. Identify the credit and debt strategy that promises to help you live a financial healthy life. Shed bad habits.

12.4.4 Asset Risks

In Chap. 7, we discussed how to manage the financial asset risks associated with building an investment portfolio. It can be done by diversifying your mix of stocks and bonds and putting the law of large numbers to work for you. As the need for funds approaches, shift out of stocks and move into relatively secure investment vehicles. U.S. Treasury bonds and money market accounts are particularly attractive. Though their rate of return is much lower today than stocks, on average, these investment vehicles will protect the value of your assets, especially from significant drops. This shift strategy reduces your exposure to those risks associated with unexpected problems in the overall economy as the need for funds approaches.

This advice is sound and works well when the economy is running smoothly. But what happens when something extraordinary happens? Consider the rippling effects of the COVID19 Crisis and the Great Recession of 2008. No one could have planned for these dips. Or could they?

During these economic downturns, the people who suffered most were those who nearing retirement with a large portion of their portfolio investments in stocks, not bonds. So, when the stock market took a dive, so did their portfolios. Plans to retire were postponed for them. Those stories made the news. What did not get covered were the stories of the people proceeded with their retirement plans because they held mostly bonds, other relatively safe assets, or cash.

Now, let's turn to the American dream of owning a home. Foreclosures skyrocketed after the housing market crashed, the Great Recession took hold, and spouses of teachers lost jobs. People walked away from homes, home projects, and gave up trying to pay on equity lines of credit. Numerous studies suggest that DTI ratios were extraordinarily high in most instances.

To avoid being caught off guard when the U.S. economy enters a recession, heed the same sound financial advice shared previously. Here are some specifics regarding homeownership:

- Treat your house as a personal asset, understanding that you have to live somewhere.
- Avoid being house rich and cash poor. Your mortgage will play an important role when calculating your debt-to-income ratio. Try to keep your ratio low. It will increase the likelihood that you can stay in your house when the economy falters or someone loses a job in your household. Avoiding a high DTI will also reduce the likelihood that you would have to sell when housing prices fall or disaster strikes.
- Do not treat your house as real asset with proceeds that can be sold to reach other financial goals. Yes, the current value of a house may contribute significantly to your total net worth (assets less liabilities, discussed in Chap. 1) but only the equity built up in your house can be used to borrow for other things. Since you are going to live somewhere and you would have to sell your house to access its value (or borrowed against), forget your house and how it figures into your financial plans in the short- or medium-term.
- Use home equity lines of credit sparingly. Borrowing against any appreciated value in your house and property can be tempting. Using credit to put on a new roof, remodeling a kitchen, or landscaping is tempting. Try to avoid the temptation. These lines of credit are still second mortgages and they necessarily increase your monthly expenses. The hope is that these projects increase the future value of your home. They may not. To minimize the risk of default, identify how you will reduce expenses in other areas of your budget or find a way to increase income before taking out a home equity line of credit.

12.5 Conclusion: Unconventional Risk Management

The death of a spouse, a serious addiction, the loss of a job, or many other things can lead us down financial paths we never anticipate. Unconventional risks are a part of life, and they cannot be eliminated. For most, there is no ordinary insurance to cover all unexpected risks. However, putting your financial house in order and having a master financial plan can take you a long way. A better prepared you is more capable of handling the downturns in life. So, build up a healthy emergency savings account, store all important documents in one place, and have some type of spending plan to more capably handle the downturns in life. So, build up a healthy emergency savings account, store all important documents in one place, and have some type of spending plan to follow when disaster strikes. An orderly financial house will provide some sense of familiarity in a sea of uncertainties.

12.6 Teacher Tipsheet on Unconventional Risk Management

- Review your budget and financial goals and make sure that they are current.
- Know where your important documents are safely placed and share information on that location with one or two highly trusted individuals.
- If you don't have a will, now is the time. Your family will be grateful if you do.
- Make sure your emergency fund account is full and have that list of bare-bone spending items close by and ready to use should you decide to go into emergency mode spending.
- Monitor your credit reports, keep on top of your debt to income ratio, and check all accounts for unusual activity. Investigate any suspicious activity as soon as possible.
- You have to live somewhere. Homeowners: Treat your houses as personal assets and refrain from borrowing against them.

12.7 Q&A

1. What are unconventional risks and how do they differ from the risks discussed so far?
   - These risks fall outside the scope of conventional risks. Unlike the risks associated with health, disability, life, and property discussed in Chap. 10, unconventional risks are largely unique and are not usually covered by ordinary insurance policies.

2. If you do not know when disaster will strike, how can you prepare for it?
   - Although you do not know the particulars, you can still have a "disaster relief" plan. Should disaster strike in your personal life, you then have contingency plans in place. Execute the one that makes the most sense given the circumstances and how they affect your income, expenses, credit and debt, assets, and debt-to-income ratio.
3. How do I get my financial house in order when a crisis occurs?
   - The short answer is that you do not. Other, more important, things will compete for your time. It is best to bring order to your financial house when there is no crisis. An orderly financial house and all that makes it up will give you breathing room to face the crisis as draw from the resources designated to be used during emergencies. This will give time to figure out how to fill any gaps in income, expense, credit, and assets. Assistance from supporters and advocacy groups can also help.

12.8   Financial 911 for Teachers

You have a financial 911 when a sudden change causes your monthly income to fall far short of your monthly expenses. We're not talking about a small auto repair; we're talking about a life-changing event such what as happened to Penelope in our opening case study. Such a financial 911 might occur because of unexpectedly high expenses, but it is more likely to happen because of sudden loss of an income (temporary or permanent). In this chapter we advised you to have a healthy emergency savings account ready, store all of your important documents in one place, and have a spending plan to follow when disaster strikes.

But what does that spending plan in the event of disaster look like? We call it a "bare-bones budget." It includes money for food, medication, and a place to live. Plus, the money it takes to keep on the lights and utilities while maintaining the transportation needed to get everyone where they need to be – you, the kids, and sitters. Almost everything else gets cut out. When you are on your bare-bones budget you do not dine out or buy yourself or others' non-necessities. That all has to wait until you're sure your financial situation has stabilized.

We recommend that you write out a bare-bones budget and keep a copy with your other important papers. That way, if disaster strikes, you'll see how little it takes just to keep going. You can then make reasoned choices about what to do next instead of panicking.

A final note: You probably have family, friends and neighbors that you would gladly help out during troubled times. You would not want them to be shy about asking. Now turn the tables. When you have your own financial 911, give others the opportunity to help you. Don't be lonely and hungry when others would love to help, visit, and bring dinner.

13

Teachers in a Market Economy

13.1 Teacher Case Study: Teaching in the Developing World

To be sure, many American schools experience significant challenges. Poverty, violence, student trauma, dysfunctional homes, and many other issues play a role in the very low achievement levels of some students in both urban and rural school districts. Acknowledging these concerns, it can be instructive to consider what education looks like in other parts of the world.

Take large parts of sub-Saharan Africa, for example. In many African nations less than one third of the population completes primary school. School is often conducted under a tree for shade and cancelled if it rains (and many of these countries experience a rainy season). More fortunate students conduct their studies in a school block – a one-room, concrete walled facility with a thatched roof, dirt floor and chalkboard. If textbooks are available, they are often obsolete and sometimes in a language the students will never master.

More troubling, even when a school block is constructed other concerns still persist. It is not uncommon for students to walk miles from their villages to their school blocks. Tragically, it is also common for the young women to be abused and even raped on the long journey.

Maria joined the Peace Corps after her graduation from a selective university's education program. She knew that she was teaching in developing country; however, she was not fully prepared for what she encountered. Schools in this part of the world commonly have pupil-teacher ratios in the neighborhood of 130:1. And salaries are very low. After adjusting for inflation and the

© The Editor(s) (if applicable) and The Author(s), under exclusive license to Springer Nature Switzerland AG 2021
T. Hunt Ferrarini et al., *Teachers Can Be Financially Fit*,
https://doi.org/10.1007/978-3-030-49356-1_13

differences in prices between the United States and impoverished African nations, a salary equivalent to a few thousand dollars per year can be expected.

Differences in standards of living between the world's rich and poor countries are extreme. To a large extent, teachers share in the general affluence or deprivation of the nations where they teach. Teachers, scholars, and policymakers might all sometimes wonder what makes some countries so rich and others so poor. Fortunately, the answer to this vexing question isn't a secret.

13.2   Natural Resources Paradox

History and geography teachers spend important class time showing their students about differences across nations in natural resources. There are nations with vast supplies of natural resources (like the United States and Canada) that are wealthy. But there are other nations with vast supplies of natural resources (like Nigeria and Venezuela) that are poor. In fact, there are nations with no natural resources (like Japan and Singapore) that are rich. Clearly, wealth is not solely a matter of natural resource endowments.

Analysts refer to the relatively poor economic performance of some resource-rich countries as the "natural resources paradox" or the "paradox of plenty." Nations that have achieved high levels of wealth share many characteristics. These characteristics have to do with their economic systems. Wealthy nations generally have economic systems that feature voluntary exchange, a price system, the profit motive, private ownership, and well-functioning financial institutions. Together, these characteristics are what economists call "market economies." Thus we can say that Singapore is wealthier than Venezuela not because of its natural resources but because of its successful market economy.

Just as economically successful nations have many characteristics in common, so too individuals who have acquired wealth in the United States share many characteristics. For example, they get a good education, live below their means, own a home, use credit cards responsibly, save regularly, and invest. In this chapter we'll have a close look at what causes individuals and nations to succeed economically.

13.3   Market Economies

Few Americans, rich or poor, spend much time wondering about the basic characteristics of our economic system. Almost certainly, they have more important things to do. Nonetheless, it might be worthwhile to pause for a few moments and consider why it is that nations such as the United States, Canada, the United Kingdom, most of the nations of Western Europe, and parts of Asia have been economically successful while other nations including many in Africa and parts of the Middle East, Latin America, and Asia, have not.

All nations have to make decisions regarding how to distribute the goods and services they produce. Different nations make these decisions in varying ways. As a market economy, the United States economy depends on prices to distribute goods and services. Rather than basing these decisions on government bureaucrats, a privileged class (like a royal family or friends of a dictator), political party affiliations, or some other method, what really matters in a market economy is willingness and ability to pay the price.

Prices, like so many things around us, often go unnoticed. We just accept them as part of the economic system. But the fact that prices are commonplace does not make them any less important. Let's explore why having a system of prices is so important to creating wealth.

13.3.1   Prices as Signals

Prices are important because they encourage voluntary exchanges for goods and services of all sorts. Prices convey complex information quickly and efficiently. They provide a basis for cooperation among strangers.

Let's turn to the core of the matter. Consider the case of Red Delicious apples grown by hundreds of Washington State's apple growers. When you buy Red Delicious apples, you don't know who produced them. Religion, race, class, and nationality don't matter. The price on the apple tells you everything you want to know. You hold the apple in your hand, look at the price, and then decide if you want to buy it.

It is much the same for the apple growers of Washington State. They don't know you. Yet they spend millions of their own dollars each year trying to produce apples that you may like to buy. Your religion, race, class, and nationality don't matter to them. Growers concentrate their attention on the price for which they can sell Red Delicious apples. If the growers do it right, they will not only be able to pay for the costs of production, they might also be able to earn a profit.

13.3.2   Prices Are Incentives

Prices provide for highly efficient communication between buyers and sellers. They tell both parties what they need to know. Imagine, for example, that pests infest the Red Delicious apple orchards in Washington. The supply of Red Delicious apples will be severely reduced. Will there be long lines at the grocery stores? Will apple eaters protest in the streets? Will grocers have to ration Red Delicious apples? No. People will calmly go about their everyday shopping. Why? Because market systems use prices to distribute products like Red Delicious apples.

Here is what will happen. The reduced supply of Red Delicious apples will cause an increase in their price. The increased price will provide an incentive to buyers to buy fewer Red Delicious apples. People who normally buy Red Delicious apples will take a sudden new interest in Granny Smiths, Braeburns, Fujis, and Galas. If some central authority were trying to decide how people should react to a reduced supply of Red Delicious apples, that authority would surely try to reduce consumption and move people toward alternatives. But the price-motivated reduction in desire for Red Delicious apples in a market economy is exactly the correct response to the problem – and it happens without a central authority issuing commands. Consumers will buy less at the new high price. Not only that: most apple buyers will do this without any knowledge of the pest invasion in Washington State. The price simply and efficiently tells apple consumers what they wanted to know about the supply of Red Delicious apples.

The increased price of Red Delicious apples also provides an incentive, encouraging other growers to get into the Red Delicious market. The opportunities for profit will be enhanced if growers can figure out how to solve the pest problem and produce more apples. This increased interest in Red Delicious apple production is exactly the correct response to the problem – again, occurring without any direction from a central authority. The price simply and efficiently tells the growers what they wanted to know about the supply of Red Delicious apples.

13.4   Voluntary Exchange: The Haircut

Market systems depend on people voluntarily making exchanges with one another. Prices are critically important in allowing voluntary exchanges to take place smoothly.

Voluntary exchanges take place because both parties see themselves as being better off as a result. Think about what happens when one of your teaching colleagues goes to his favorite barber for a haircut. The barber cuts his hair and says, "That will be $15.00 please." The customer looks in the mirror, nods his satisfaction, and hands over the money. Depending on local custom, there may also be a generous tip. The barber says, "Thank you, and please come back again." The customers says, "Thank you, I'll see you in a few weeks." This is voluntary exchange. Voluntary exchange takes place millions of times every day and we scarcely notice. Both sides gain and that explains why we spend so much time thanking one another.

Why the big deal about voluntary exchange? Think about how it could be different. What if people were forced to provide goods and services? Consider our nation's tragic history of slavery, a difficult subject dealt with by your fellow teachers in the social studies. Slavery was a denial of voluntary exchange. People ordinarily "own" their capacity for labor. It is their most valuable and important resource. If they choose to use it on behalf of others, they expect to get something in return. They expect to be paid.

But slavery created a legal system that sanctioned stealing labor from one person and giving it to another. This system of legalized theft violated a principle of private ownership: the principle that people own their own labor. It was not a market system based on voluntary exchange. It was a system that depended on non-voluntary exchanges, coercively enforced.

13.5   The Profit Motive

Why do businesses work so hard to please us with the latest products and services we desire? It turns out that while we enjoy the benefits of the hard work of others, they are doing it with their own incomes and families in mind. By running successful businesses (earning a profit), they can buy that new home, put their children through college, or take care of others that are less fortunate.

13.5.1   Private Ownership

Private ownership helps in ways that may be less obvious. Economists often say, "There is no such thing as a free lunch." By this they mean that all of us (individuals, families, cities, nations) face scarcity. We desire more goods and services than our time, skills, labor, capital, and natural resources permit us to obtain. By allowing most resources to be owned privately, we provide an incentive for people to use them in the most efficient way possible. Not only can businesses be built, so can homes, apartments, schools, parks hospitals, roads, and churches.

Not only can we take care of our own families, we can have resources left over to address other improvement goals – defending our nation from attack, improving the environment, building a better transportation system, and so on. These common goals are addressed through government. Some of these goals, including national defense, are difficult even to imagine providing without government. But while governments have a unique ability to work toward common goals, they may struggle to provide good customer service when the goals are smaller. In such cases government often does not produce benefits of the sort we find produced in the private sector. Many examples exist. Think about the last time you renewed your driver's license at the Department of Motor Vehicles. If your experience was like that of many DMV customers, you were required to pull a number, wait in long lines, complete many forms, and work with grumpy clerks. How long could a business survive with competition if it dealt with customers the same way?

To some people *profit* is a dirty word. To these folks, the quest for profits is little more than an expression of greed. And it is no secret that some people are, indeed, greedy. But selfish behavior is not only found among profit-seeking business people. Selfishness and greed are also traits we sometimes find in lawyers, teachers, scientists, ministers, and elected officials. It is a common human trait.

How do market economies address the potential of business people to act in greedy ways? Why don't all businesses strive to "rip off" their customers to earn a large profit? In part because businesses are regulated against fraud, price-fixing, and other illegal activity. But a more powerful incentive against acting in this manner is their competitors. Any business that treats its customers poorly runs the risk of losing business to competing firms. Therefore, a key role for government is to assure that there is plenty of competition throughout the many different parts of the economy.

13.5.2   Economic Institutions

The vast majority of people who become wealthy in the United States do so because they have decided to accept the opportunities offered by our economy. One of the most important ways to start building wealth is to establish a relationship with a financial institution. Simply by establishing a connection to a bank, for example, individuals can help themselves while helping others.

The United States provides its people with a system of stable and well-regulated financial institutions. Let's focus on banks for a moment. By enabling people to place some of their earnings into savings accounts, banks reward saving. Individuals benefit from saving, obviously. But there is more to the story. Money saved by individuals is used, in turn, to provide loans to others. Loans are often made to business owners. These loans can be used to expand existing businesses or open new ones. These loans can also be used to build new homes and purchase goods and services that people want. As this money circulates, getting put to new uses, it results in jobs and opportunities for others. Many poor countries, like those profiled in the opening case study, lack such strong economic institutions and even the secure rule of law required to develop them.

13.6   Why Do People Make What They Make?

Millions of people in our market economy have market-determined wages and salaries. For these people, knowing about prices, voluntary exchange, and the profit motive is important in understanding why some earn more money than others. In addition to those with market-determined wages and salaries, there are millions more whose pay is set by an administrative process (such as the adoption of a teacher salary scale by a school board). Here the market has a background role.

However wages and salaries are set, nearly everyone thinks they are worth more than they are paid. Just ask them. Economists approach the subject differently. They begin with a focus on the market for labor. To work correctly, markets depend on prices. And the prices in labor markets are wages and salaries.

For people with market-determined salaries, income depends directly on the productive resources they own and the amount of money those resources can fetch in the marketplace. For most of us, our income depends on wages and salaries. The wage or salary paid to a worker is a reflection of the market price for his or her labor. It reflects how much businesses are willing and able to offer for that labor. It also reflects how much workers are willing to accept. For business owners, their income is the difference between how much money they receive from customer sales and how much they spend in producing goods and services.

For people with administratively set salaries, pay depends on the relative strength of employers and employees. Employees with effective collective bargaining agreements will receive more pay, while employees with little organization and few alternatives will receive less. Even with administratively set salaries, however, the market has an influence. When teachers are leaving a school system for higher pay elsewhere, even a school board not inclined to raise pay may find that it must compete to attract and retain teachers. Thus competition plays a role even when pay is set administratively.

13.7   Labor Markets

In order to compete successfully in labor markets, individuals must have something of value to offer to others. Most people increase the skills they can offer by improving their levels of education and training. Economists call investments in education and training improvements in human capital.

How can individuals increase their value to those that want to hire? Education is the simple and most powerful answer. In general, it is the lack of education and training that results in low-paying jobs. Other factors, of course, also influence labor markets and people's income.

- People with more skills and more experience, and those who work harder, are more valuable to employers and are more likely to receive higher wages and salaries.
- People who are middle-aged tend to earn more income than people who are young. Older workers generally have more knowledge, skills, and experience.
- Some people are luckier than others. Natural abilities such as strength, good looks, coordination, intelligence, and so on are all factors that may have a bearing on income. Some people inherit money. Others can throw a baseball 90 miles per hour.

Like other markets, markets for labor are dynamic. For example, demand for software engineers is likely to increase faster in the near future than the demand for other workers. Demand for machinists is likely to decrease, compared to the demand for other workers. Similarly, the supply of workers influences the market price of labor. You may notice in your own occupation how difficult it is for your school district to find well-qualified math and science teachers, and yet they receive many applicants for teaching at the primary grades. Once again, administratively set salaries—while not determined directly by the market—are influenced by market forces such as competition and scarcity.

13.8   How to Increase Your Income

Since many teachers' pay is set administratively, they don't just become more productive and get hired away in a marketplace. Instead they must persuade a principal or superintendent that their pay is too low. There are a couple of time-tested hints that might help you make this case. Be courteous, gather information on competing school districts, emphasize how you love your job and want to keep working for your community. Take on tasks that others are not interested in because they are difficult or time consuming. Be known as a teacher that "says yes" when called upon with a new challenge. All of these acts will provide you with the best chance to be considered for a salary increase when the funds are available.

One can also think about two different paths to increasing your salary as a teacher. The first involves improving your own human capital (through additional education and training) and being prepared to move if necessary. The move may not require relocating your residence but you might need to move to a different school district that is willing to offer you a higher salary for your new skills. A second path to higher pay is to work collectively with other teachers to increase your school system's salary scales. Here you are subject to a free-rider problem – you do the work and colleagues who did nothing will typically benefit also. This can be a long road that may become contentious with the administrators in your building, with your school board, and potentially even with members of the community. This isn't to say it's not worth pursuing; however, if you choose to go this route, understand it is likely to take a significant amount of time and effort and there is no guarantee of success.

13.9   Conclusion: The Market Economy

Understanding and participating in the market economy offers the greatest chance for people to succeed. Admirers and critics agree that market systems create wealth. One reason for their success is that markets are congruent with human nature. Over time, they provide rewards and, at the same time, produce many public benefits. To succeed economically, nations require the following:

• Widespread private ownership and use of the profit motive to reward enterprise, self-reliance, and responsibility.

- Active competition to impose discipline on business owners and make them efficient and productive.
- A system of free market prices and voluntary exchange to promote cooperation among people.
- Competitive labor markets to encourage hiring of the best and most productive people, with an educational system that promotes human capital formation among all of its students.
- Strong economic institutions like banks and financial markets that require proper government regulation and the rule of law.

To the extent that these conditions are in place, people see improvements in their standard of living. Market systems certainly are not perfect, but overall we have not been able to come up with a better system. It only took economists more than 300 years to figure this all out!

13.10   Teacher Tipsheet on Participating in a Market Economy

- It can difficult for most Americans to recognize how drastically living standards differ around the world. At times it may feel like you earn a relatively low income compared to others. Don't forget about the amazing opportunities available to you by participating fully in the vibrant American economy.
- Prices are a very powerful incentive that contain lots of important information. As you evaluate economic opportunities remember that high prices are paid for goods or services in scarce supply. This should tell you something important about your opportunities.
- Labor markets match jobs and job seekers using wages and prices. One way to improve your economic success is to increase your productivity through training and education.
- Even when wages and salaries are administratively set, being productive and adding in-demand skills can increase your income.
- In general, our economy is built around voluntary exchange. In order to get ahead economically you need to offer something to others that they will voluntarily pay for.
- Understanding how our market economy works is important for all citizens. But it is especially important for those interested in getting ahead financially.

13.11   Q&A

1. Do natural resources explain the differences in living standards around the world?
   - No. There are examples of nations with rich endowments of natural resources that are both rich and poor. And nations without natural resources can be rich or poor. A nation's standard of living has more to do with its economic systems. The vast majority of wealthy countries have market-oriented economies that include private property protection, the profit motive, free trade, limited government, economic institutions, and respect for the rule of law.
2. Does my teaching salary reflect what I am worth?
   - No. In our legal and ethical system, human worth is inherent and not defined by how much someone is paid. However, a teaching salary does reflect the supply and demand for teachers in your area, as filtered through your school district's institutions, salary setting procedures and possible collective bargaining agreements.
3. Teaching second grade is clearly a more important job than playing professional basketball. Why do I made so much less money than NBA players?
   - Unfortunately, incomes are not determined by the importance of a job. Rather, incomes are based on the scarcity of skills required to perform a particular job. Very few people throw a baseball at 100 miles an hour, can play quarterback in the NFL successfully, or can compete on the basketball court against the world's best athletes. Because of the scarcity of such skills, professional athletes are highly compensated. While teaching students is an important job, it turns out many people have the skills and desire to do it successfully.
4. Why are prices so important to a well-functioning market economy?
   - Prices act as signals of value. They help consumers determine when to economize and cut back on their spending. They also send a signal to producers that they should increase production of something consumers want.

13.12   Financial 911 for Teachers

You have a financial 911 when the skills and education you have obtained are no longer in demand by employers. This kind of financial 911 might not happen suddenly. Unlike a teacher strike or government budget glitch that might catch you off guard, this situation can be anticipated. You will probably see it coming. That gives you time to adapt if you find the subjects you're teaching are in decline.

A reason that market economies are so efficient and vibrant is that they can quickly adapt to changing circumstances. In a process called "creative destruction" the economy is always eliminating businesses we no longer desire (VHS movie rentals, for example) and replacing them with what we do want (movie rental through streaming services).

One of the wonderful things about a career in teaching is that it is less susceptible to market forces. Teachers are employed in every city and town, and it is hard to imagine a machine replacing the need for teachers. In this way, teaching is different from manufacturing or many service-oriented occupations. However, you have likely noticed the trend toward online education and other technological solutions that may allow many more students to be taught by a single teacher. It is also true that some areas of teaching have become nearly obsolete (keyboarding, home economics, some types of shop classes, Latin instruction, and driver's education) while others have surged in popularity (computer science, Mandarin Chinese).

If you find yourself teaching in an area that is decreasing in demand, it may make sense to pursue additional training. It is often relatively easy to obtain another area of teaching certification once you already have a degree in education. Think about the needs of the future and act before the labor market changes in a way that may damage your career.

14

Don't Keep It a Secret

14.1 Teacher Case Study: Anthony's Story Shows How Teaching Can Change Lives

What does it mean to be happy in life? Is it just about wealth and finances? Of course, it is not. We hear stories about lottery winners. Yes, the initial windfall of millions of dollars does inject a ton of good things into the lives of the winners. Eventually their whole lives return to where they were prior to winning, but with a great deal of financial worries and stress in between.

Happiness involves much, much more than a career and money. It includes a journey toward purpose and meaning in life. Money has value because it opens opportunities on that journey. Consider the story of Anthony – a middle school student living in poverty with his immigrant mother who neither spoke English nor had easily employable skills.

Anthony's teachers committed to experiential learning through principled entrepreneurship throughout their school. They adopted programs and market activities that gave their students sound money management skills, demonstrated how to run successful businesses through principled entrepreneurship, and invited local businesses owners and industry leaders to talk about the importance of education and how it's valued in competitive markets.

The teachers' efforts paid off. Anthony went on to finish high school while running his own business. He organized a band, became its lead singer, and marketed it. Eventually, the band gained in popularity attracting people from all over. Anthony sold t-shirts to concert goers and launched offshoot businesses. Much later, he went on to become a multi-millionaire. Anthony

© The Editor(s) (if applicable) and The Author(s), under exclusive license to Springer Nature   **155**
Switzerland AG 2021
T. Hunt Ferrarini et al., *Teachers Can Be Financially Fit*,
https://doi.org/10.1007/978-3-030-49356-1_14

credits his success to his immigrant mom who took risks, a strong education that placed experiential learning at its center, and his teachers who made magic happen.

14.2   About Teaching Students to Be Financially Fit and Available Resources

What you do in the classroom and at school matters. You know that. Other professionals admire your passion and commitment to the future. They understand and respect the sacrifices you make in order to educate today's students and prepare tomorrow's leaders.

Continue to do what you do best! That is, set the stage for others to succeed in life through education, including finances. Here are some resources to support your educational efforts, extending your reach beyond the classroom. All resources mentioned are high quality, teacher tested, and student approved.

14.3   Teach Others About Financial Fundamentals: Resources

Teachers want students to be successful, not only in their classrooms but beyond. As discussed throughout this book, well-rounded success includes whole life success, of which financial fitness is only one part. But, the two are intertwined.

Individuals who develop the habits of working diligently, setting firm goals and achieving them, continuing to march forward to complete a mission even with setbacks, and avoiding temptations of instant gratification are the people who typically who experience success. That is, they get what they want, frequently get more than they expect, and have a tendency to include a lot of other people through their own earned success.

There is a plethora of high quality resources available for K-12 and postsecondary use. They are dedicated to helping teachers impart financial knowledge and give students practice making sound decisions in their classrooms. Through the educational process, students can form good habits, acquire marketable skills, and make solid connections between what happens in their classrooms and the outside world. Available resources take students through developing sound financial habits, connecting career options to education, using economics to connect income opportunities and occupations, and financial planning for life.

As a teacher, you can start small with a classroom activity or go big with an entire curriculum. Below is a list of quality resources tied to financial literacy standards and benchmarks. Each is created by specialists in the field with the help of educational experts and academics well-researched in the content areas. Unless noted, resources are available at no money cost.

14.3.1 Council on Economic Education Resources

The *Council on Economic Education* provides a wide variety of personal finance resources. Only a few are mentioned here. *EconEdLink.org* (https://www.econedlink.org) supplies a wide range of online lesson plans, activities, simulators, and videos. They are classroom ready and do not involve large commitments of class time or teacher investments. Sign up for a teacher's account and keep all of your favorites in one spot.

Teachers looking for a full curriculum can adopt *Learning, Earning and Investing* *Lessons for a New Generation* (http://lei.councilforeconed.org) or *Financial Fitness for Life* *(FFFL)* (http://fffl.councilforeconed.org). These both offer action-oriented lessons intended to reinforce key concepts and topics.

Learning, Earning and Investing backs up the Stock Market Game™ sponsored by the securities industry. The game is built on an investing competition. This online simulation spreads across global markets and asks students in grades 4–12 to apply economic reasoning to explore investing and personal finance in the modern world. Many of the lessons move well beyond the competition. Lessons and practical applications explore the connections between well-diversified investments and investments in human capital (education), earning potential, and careers promising overall financial security and supporting comfortable lifestyles.

Financial Fitness for Life provides more general and broader coverage. It includes K-12 teacher and parent guides and student workbooks on how to illustrate the connections between sound financial habits and healthy and wealthy financial living. This curriculum is available in Spanish. Details and pricing information for these and other Council on Economic Education programs are located at the Council's store (https://store.councilforeconed.org/).

National Personal Finance Challenge (https://www.councilforeconed.org/npfc/) provides an opportunity for students in grades 6–12 to build knowledge, make choices, form habits, gain experiences connecting how different economic events influence financial outcomes based on personal choices and habits, and identify how sound decisions and behaviors lead to better outcomes. Students compete at state levels. Winners move on to nationals. Teams are made up of diverse set of students with widely diverse backgrounds and a very broad range of academic and career interests.

14.3.2 Federal Reserve System Resources

The *Federal Reserve System* (https://www.federalreserveeducation.org/) provides a wide variety of rich K-12 and college resources. This system connects the program and resources supplied by the twelve regional Federal Reserve Banks. *Econ Ed at the Fed St. Louis* (https://www.stlouisfed.org/education) offers links to simulators, videos, podcasts, and online courses and assignments for students and teachers. It supports an online platform called *EconLowDown* (https://www.econlowdown.org/) which makes free online courses and videos available to K-12 classrooms and colleges. Hundreds of high-quality resources are easy to find once registered users securely enter the platform. A wide variety of student-centered, highly engaging activities exist alongside stand-alone assignments and full programs. Programs include *The Keys to Financial Success* and *Making Finance Personal: Project-Based Learning for the Personal Finance Classroom.* Teachers and schools can also get posters, infographics, workbooks, and other materials delivered to classrooms at no money cost. If interested, a growing number of materials are available in Spanish and more materials aimed at involving parents are coming into the system.

14.3.3 Junior Achievement Resources

Junior Achievement° (https://www.juniorachievement.org) celebrated its centennial in 2019. This non-profit organization has the longest history of dedication to the cause of effectively advancing financial literacy, work readiness, and entrepreneurship. JA has four programs - JA Personal Finance°, JA Economics for Success°, JA Finance Park°, and JA Finance Park° Virtual. Its programs differentiate themselves from others by engaging volunteers and using them to present, lead activities, and share stories. Students make connections with others' lives and gain the ability to navigate various twists and turns by remaining true to a few key financial habits. Volunteers and their shared experiences reinforce what teachers teach on developing strong financial discipline and planning for a future that includes successful and comfortable financial lives. JA products and programs involve a price and are launched through regional offices.

14.3.4 Other Resources

Jump$tart Coalition˙ for Personal Financial (https://www.jumpstart.org/) provides its own excellent programs similar to those mentioned above. Unique to Jump$tart is its clearinghouse for financial literacy resources. The *Jump$tart Clearinghouse* (https://jumpstartclearinghouse.org) provides relatively quick access to various teacher training opportunities, and links to a wide variety of young adult resources for independent learners. Find out what is available, when it was produced, and check out reviews.

Next Gen Personal Finance (https://www.ngpf.org/) provides everything needed to teach personal finance in a time slot as short as one 30-minute class or as long as a full semester. It has Google-based programs with documents that are well-suited for Google Classrooms but everything is adaptable for other classrooms. Next Gen excels in providing case studies, creating assignments require the use of spreadsheets to make calculations, and providing information about what is available, what's new, and how to link current events to their materials through social media, especially Twitter and Facebook. Next Gen additionally makes assessment materials available through Kahoot, Quizlet Deck, and Quizziz.

The National Endowment for Financial Education˙ offers a *High School Financial Planning Program˙* (https://www.nefe.org). It boasts about being a "turnkey financial literacy program," targeting teens and providing resources for both teachers and parents. NEFE provides research funds for interested parties interested in exploring the topic of personal finance and all of its parts. A wide range of materials are available for educators interested in instructing their students actively using materials heavily influenced by scholarly research.

14.4 Teachers Engaging Parents

"Parents are the greatest influence on young adult financial behaviors," according to the research of the National Endowment for Financial Education˙ (National Endowment for Financial Education 2020). Jump$tart and the Council on Economic Education concur. The Council's Survey of the States provides evidence, finding that most states do not require teaching personal finance and among the states that do, not all require testing. This dampens some teachers' willingness to dedicate class time to personal finance. If you are reading this book, you are likely not among those that choose not to teach about finances. If you are, you can still help out in the effort to advance financial literacy in the K-16 school systems by engaging parents.

Parents are front and center when it comes to advancing financial literacy and helping young people develop positive money habits and financial attitudes. Turn to parents and let them increase student awareness about important financial matters. Encourage parents to help their children by sharing own their financial experiences and lessons they learned along the way with their children. Provide parents with resources to help their children develop positive financial habits, attitudes, and aptitudes. Here are some things you can do:

- Provide personal finance assignments to be completed by students and their parents.
- Host a "classroom" activity that includes a parent-participation element, possibly on Parents' night.
- Commuicate with parents about what is happening in class. Supply information and links to activities on how parents can join their students and learn more about key topics. Invite parents to observe class and encourage those with expertise and stories to present or volunteer.
- Encourage parents to reinforce what is taught in the classroom. Invite them to explore opportunities to complement in-school activites with at-home exercises. Econ Ed at the St. Louis Fed and National Endowment for Financial Education˚ (NEFE˚) designed materials specifically for parents with these interests.
- Educate parents along with students. Host a Facebook page or send out emails that invite parents to learn along with their students.
- Make parents aware of the importance of teaching their children about money management, explaining that their children or others will be partly responsible for their elderly care, balancing their investment portfolios, and managing their finance during retirement.

14.5 Teachers Helping Other Teachers and Others in Their Schools

Teachers committed to weaving financial education into their courses across the curriculum and content areas are discovering creative ways to help their comrades. Here are a few ideas.

1. Launch a monthly lunch-and-learn financial fitness series. Invite others to join you with a brown bag lunch to discuss the practical elements of sound financial thinking. (For a nice step up, see if a local financial institution will sponsor lunch.) Bring in parents who budget, local financial advisors, well-known and successful business persons, or someone from human resources to talk about different topics.
2. Start an investment club. An internet search on "How to start an investment club" provides a wide range of possibilities. Buddy up with another teacher, parent, or an expert, and create a "club" that best fits the personality of the targeted group.
3. Launch a savings challenge at school. Help others ease into the habit of savings. Numerous examples exist online. Search for "52 week savings challenge," and invite others to join you.
4. Celebrate Financial Literacy month. Identify a list of things to do across classrooms that connect the importance of financial fitness to healthy and wealthy living. The month of April is often designated the official month to celebrate Financial Literacy by state councils on financial literacy and national organizations such as JumpStart. Feel free to select any month or start with one day per term.
5. Take an online course with others. A variety of courses exist. You can complete "Practical Personal Finance" on Canvas.net and earn a badge in about 2–3 h after successfully navigating through collected materials and completing interactives and quizzes on the 12 key elements of sound thinking about practical personal finance. Or, you can take a deep dive into individual topics, ranging from budgeting basics to retirement planning to exploring insurance options. Money Strands (https://moneystrands.com/) and the Federal Reserve Bank of St. Louis offer both not-for-credit and for-credit courses.
6. Attend a workshop on financial literacy for adults or teachers. Find a local event. Invite someone to attend with you.

14.6 Conclusion

From kindergarten through high school and adult audiences, everyone can be taught about money matters. Age, income, background, and occupational interests do not matter. Since the topics of personal finance can be foreign, abstract, and complex, carefully select resources and structure events that promise to excite and engage you and others in what it means to be financial fit. Financial fitness opens financial possibilities and income earning opportunities that may otherwise be closed. Once the key connection between sound money habits and successful living through purposeful spending, regular savings, diversified investment, and strategic debt is made, strong comfortable and secure living can commence. As described above, high quality stand-alone programs, lesson plans, interactives, simulators, challenges, clubs, and other resources exist at no or little money cost to you. Step back. Look at what is available. Find what will most likely work best given your audience. Grab it. Customize it to include practical examples and relevant activities that are likely to resonate with your audience. Now that you are ready and set, go. Promise us, the authors, that you will enjoy the journey. Happy days to you and the people you inspire!

14.7   Teacher Tipsheet: Don't Keep It a Secret

- Bring financial education into the classroom. Start with a short activity. Consider an entire program in the future.
- Check out the numerous resources that are available. Many of them are provided without cost to you.
- Educate yourself and help others learn more about developing sound financial habits that will help build character and set the state for living comfortably and securely.
- Engage parents. They're a great resource and often willing to help, if only someone will ask.
- Collaborate with others in your department and throughout your school. Helping others with financial matters in turn provides overall satisfaction and contributes to your own happy living.

14.8   Q&A

1. Why are people giving away financial education resources? Do they have an axe to grind or a particular viewpoint to favor in their free materials?
   - It's good to look out for a particular viewpoint in materials given away free – you already know that as a teacher. In personal finance education, for example, banks want their industry and the practice of banking to look good. However, that doesn't make their checking account activities

any less valuable for students. Also note that national nonprofits such as the Council for Economic Education and Junior Achievement have a primarily educational mission and do not endorse specific providers of financial services in their materials. Use the judgment you have developed as a teacher and you'll be fine.

2. Do you, the authors, have a "short list" of principles that can be used across a variety of different audiences?

   – Here's a short list of three good concepts that cover a lot of what we talk about in this book:

   (i)   First, money earned is money given in exchange for providing services to others. It is saved and spent more carefully and purposefully than money received as a gift or transferred from one person to another through unemployment, Social Security, or another government-sponsored program.

   (ii) Second, money both helps us get what we want, AND it helps others get what they want.

   (iii) Third, the most important single thing you can do is to spend less than you earn. That gives you the room to save and invest regularly and purposefully to take advantage of compounding. (If you don't spend less than you earn, the only goal you'll every accomplish is spending.)

3. Is there a common key to financial success that would apply across children, teachers, parents, business people – and even nations?

   – Yes. Financial success is achieved in the same way by all of these parties. It is realized by setting goals, budgeting and saving regularly, using credit prudently, consuming wisely, investing strategically, and working purposefully in order to live comfortably and securely. All of these goals must be kept in balance with each other.

4. Is there any one tool that is the most valuable in teaching others to gain control over their finances so their finances don't gain control over them?

   – There are many possibilities, but our favorite is zero-based budgeting that requires every dollar spent to be matched against a financial goal and linked to income. It requires everyone to spend limited income and shows that more spending in one area translates to less spending in another today or in the future.

14.9   Financial 911 for Teachers

Now that we're at the end of our Financial 911s for teachers, we would like to pass along a few general tips about how to help fellow teachers in trouble. In previous chapters our 911s dealt with specific subjects. This chapter-ending advice is more about relationships.

When you see a fellow teacher showing signs of financial stress, such as drowning in student debt, lend an ear. In a quiet space and ever so gently, offer to sit down and chat. Listen without judgment. Recognize the heaviness of the situation. At the same time, offer hope and extend a helping hand. There are teachers out there who have successfully addressed their debt problems along with resolving a host of other financial issues. Although there is not one solution that fits every situation, there are numerous options that are tied together by sound financial behaviors and habits. Talk in broad terms, using much of what is provided in this book and available online.

Do not try to remake your colleague's financial life in just one session. Instead, ask your colleague to meet again. This time, return with some success stories that relate in some way to the situation at hand. They are available online. Their purpose will be to inspire and motivate your friend to take next steps with hope of success. When the time is right, encourage your colleague to focus on taking broad financial steps that lead to secure and comfortable living. Nudge them to start by putting together a budget. Stress the importance of placing all expense, credit, retirement, and income information in one place and using that central location, the budget, as a place to get a handle on the crisis, find solutions to move through the crisis, and set the stage for a lifetime of happiness. The goal is to make the current crisis become a blip from which one learned important lessons on the way to financially healthy living.

Regardless of progress on the crisis front or putting together a complete budget, congratulate your colleague the next time you meet on whatever steps have been taken. Shift attention to developing a life plan. If appropriate, point your colleague to contact a local professional with expertise, enter an online program, or work with a trusted advisor that can help tackle the problem at hand in the context of a whole life plan. If not appropriate, continue to offer to meet occasionally, show a willingness to lend an ear, and offer support by sharing relevant resources on sound money management.

If progress is slow and it seems that all you're doing is offering a sympathetic ear, do not minimize the importance of that. Sometimes we all need someone to listen more than anything else.

Reference

National Endowment for Financial Education (2020) Parents play a critical role in financial education. https://www.hsfpp.org/about/parents.aspx. Accessed 6 April 2020.

Index

CPSIA information can be obtained
at www.ICGtesting.com
Printed in the USA
LVHW060936120423
744047LV00002BA/6

9 783030 493554

Tawni Hunt Ferrarini · M. Scott Niederjohn · Mark C. Schug · William C. Wood

Teachers Can Be Financially Fit
Economists' Advice for Educators

This book uses relatable case studies to dispense practical financial advice to educators. Written by an expert team of four award-winning economic educators, the book provides an engaging narrative specifically designed for teachers and their unique financial needs.

Educators are attracted to the teaching profession for numerous reasons. Prospective teachers enter the profession believing it offers a certain level of job security and good benefits, usually including a defined-benefit, state-funded pension. But things are changing. Pensions vary widely from state to state and even within school districts. Many private schools do not offer even basic 403(b) saving plans and, when they do, they are often not very generous. Much the same can be said of many charter schools and private colleges and universities.

The book consists of fourteen chapters covering a comprehensive group of topics specifically curated for educators teaching at the K-12 and university level, including saving for retirement, managing debt, investment strategies, and real estate. Each chapter begins with a case study of an educator in a specific financial situation, which sets the scene for the introduction and explanation of key concepts. The chapters include a Q&A section to address common questions and conclude with a "Financial 911" focusing on a financial emergency related to the chapter topic.

ISBN 978-3-030-49355-4

▶ springer.com